The Salvation Enigma

The Salvation Enigma

By Alexander M. Frazier

Greenville, SC

The Salvation Enigma

Copyright © 2017 by Alexander M. Frazier

All rights reserved.

Alexander M. Frazier, Mauldin 29662.

ISBN 978-0-692-93387-9 (Trade Paperback)

First Edition: September 2017

Printed in the United States of America

Contents

Preface vii

Acknowledgements ix

Abbreviations xi

1 – The Plan 1

2 – The Law 16

3 – The Oath 28

4 – The Relationship 40

5 – The Annulling 54

6 – The Ä′gə-pā′ Principle 68

7 – Ancillary Issues 84

8 – A Call to Action 100

Preface

The purpose of this work is to explain the intricacies of how salvation functions in a technical sense. While the individual pieces of this puzzle are common knowledge to most Christians who engage in any study or discussion, it has been my observation that organizing them coherently to see the full picture is a more elusive task than one might expect.

Because this work delves into the mechanical workings of salvation, it does, by necessity, touch on several controversial topics as a matter of context. Certain instances required me to take a definitive position relative to whatever point I was making. However, it is neither the goal of this book, nor the purpose, to argue doctrine, and I did take great pains to avoid doing so as much as possible, tempting though it was on several occasions.

Let me also state that the structure of the work is systematic. For my readers to gain a comprehensive understanding of the general topic, it was needful to lay out the individual components before combining them. By analogy, it is like discussing red and yellow before explaining the color orange. Most doctrines overlap and are interdependent. There is the law, and there is grace. There is faith, and there is works. Before any doctrines can be fully harmonized, they first have to be discussed in their basest state. So as a speaker at a lecture might say, "please hold your questions 'til the end." You will likely discover that any objections you may have are addressed as you read through.

Lastly, the conclusions presented in this work are absolutely orthodox. No new doctrines have been introduced. I have merely shown how the known doctrines work together as a whole, whereas they are usually taught more or less either autonomously, or in their smaller groupings and relationships. In this sense, the conclusions of this work, though not necessarily its individual parts, will be new territory for most.

For those who find that faith is enough, this book may be little more than a curiosity. There is certainly good information to be had if you choose to read it through. For those who want answers, I've provided them, at least where this topic is concerned. I do hope and pray that this work will be a blessing to you, and provide you a foundation of understanding that will illuminate so many more things.

Acknowledgements

For their assistance in helping me fine-tune the arguments, and for the hours they've spent reading, proofing, and critiquing this work for accuracy, continuity, and scriptural integrity, I wanted to offer my appreciation to the following:

Ben Shanks, Don Bessinger, Jason Mele, Dedrick Smith, and Justin Davis.

Bible Abbreviations

Gen.	Genesis	Nah.	Nahum
Exod.	Exodus	Hab.	Habakkuk
Lev.	Leviticus	Zeph.	Zephaniah
Num.	Numbers	Hag.	Haggai
Deut.	Deuteronomy	Zech.	Zechariah
Josh.	Joshua	Mal.	Malachi
Judg.	Judges	Matt.	Matthew
Ruth	Ruth	Mk.	Mark
1 Sam.	1 Samuel	Lk.	Luke
2 Sam.	2 Samuel	Jn.	John
1 Kgs.	1 Kings	Acts	Acts
2 Kgs.	2 Kings	Rom.	Romans
1 Chr.	1 Chronicles	1 Cor.	1 Corinthians
2 Chr.	2 Chronicles	2 Cor.	2 Corinthians
Ezra	Ezra	Gal.	Galatians
Neh.	Nehemiah	Eph.	Ephesians
Est.	Esther	Phil.	Philippians
Job	Job	Col.	Colossians
Ps.	Psalms	1 Thes.	1 Thessalonians
Prov.	Proverbs	2 Thes.	2 Thessalonians
Eccl.	Ecclesiastes	1 Tim.	1 Timothy
Song of Sol.	Song of Solomon	2 Tim.	2 Timothy
Isa.	Isaiah	Ti.	Titus
Jer.	Jeremiah	Philem.	Philemon
Lam.	Lamentations	Heb.	Hebrews
Ezek.	Ezekiel	Jas.	James
Dan.	Daniel	1 Pet.	1 Peter
Hos.	Hosea	2 Pet.	2 Peter
Joel	Joel	1 Jn.	1 John
Amos	Amos	2 Jn.	2 John
Obad.	Obadiah	3 Jn.	3 John
Jon.	Jonah	Jude	Jude
Mic.	Micah	Rev.	Revelation

1

The Plan

Biblical salvation is a peculiar thing. Most of us know we are saved. Some of us can even remember the day or date we gave our lives to Christ. But after decades' worth of conversations on the topic, I can tell you with absolute certainty that the average Christian typically has no idea what salvation is, how it works, or what practical effect it has on us. The questions so often asked by Christians of all levels of spiritual maturity make this abundantly clear. People debate whether or not we need to keep the Law of Moses. They argue about whether we are predestined by God, or if our own free will plays a part. They even wonder whether salvation can be lost, or if it is eternally secure once obtained. These, and many other controversial topics, are easily put to rest with a competent understanding of our salvation and how it functions.

For that reason, it has been on my heart to write this book for some time. I want you to understand your salvation, and through that understanding come to see what it really means to be a Christian. I want you to know why it wasn't enough — indeed, why it wasn't even possible — for God to simply say, "I forgive you," and let that be the end of it. I want you to know why it was necessary for Jesus to lay his life on the line and die on the cross to accomplish the gift that is our salvation.

That being said, the best place to start is with the plan, which is not only the logical starting place, but also a foundational concept of scripture that I have found to be amongst the most misunderstood. Although it is plainly stated in scripture, most have no idea what it is.

The general view of mainstream Christianity tends to be in agreement with the ideas of dispensationalism, which is the theory that our biblical history has been a series of redemptive covenants following the fall, each successively designed to facilitate a reconciliation with God. As the teaching goes, God created Adam sinless and innocent, and his will was for Adam to live forever in the paradise of the Garden of Eden. But Adam and Eve, beguiled by the serpent's lie, ate from the tree of the knowledge of good and evil. In so doing, they went against God's will and violated the only commandment they were given, bringing death upon themselves and ruination to God's perfect plan.

Separated from us by sin, but not wanting to forsake his creation, God crafted a new plan by which he might bring mankind back to himself.[1] When that plan failed, he gave us another. And when that one failed, he gave us yet another. For centuries, mankind struggled through the many trials of conscience, human government, the written law, and other

---

1. Isa. 59:2. Isaiah doesn't say that a single sin makes God unable to hear us. It says that God turned his back on Israel in anger because of her constant sin.

covenants, each intended to offer redemption and life, but that each failed because of man's depravity.[1]

In the end, God ultimately sent his only begotten son to die when all other attempts at reconciliation had failed.

This, in a nutshell, is the gist of what most Christians believe. Certain details may differ, but the foundation is more or less the same. That is to say, Christians tend to believe in the absurd notion that we mere mortals have managed to repeatedly thwart the majestic plans of an all-powerful God through our arbitrary acts of disobedience, forcing him time and again to alter his plans to accommodate our wickedness.

This dispensational mentality, which is greatly expounded upon in academic circles, is most readily personified by the Old Covenant versus New Covenant dynamic we are all so familiar with. They are perceived as autonomous covenants, each with the independent goal of reconciling us to God. Because the one covenant failed due to our weakness, the other covenant was given. It is the epitome of the dispensational model.

However, while there *are* some facets of the Old versus

---

1. Berkhof, *Systematic Theology*, 290. The notion of multiple plans is most commonly, though not exclusively, taught as part of dispensational theology. The number of dispensations ranges from as few as two (New Covenant and Old Covenant) to as many as seven. By name, they are *Innocence*, *Conscience*, *Human Government*, *Promise*, the *Law*, *Grace*, and the *Kingdom*. As Scofield states, "Each of the dispensations may be regarded as a new test of the natural man, and each ends in judgment, — marking his failure." Frank E. Gaebelein also states, "… Instead of casting off his guilty creature, God was moved with compassion, and gave him a fresh trial under new conditions. Thus each dispensation ends with failure, and each dispensation shows forth God's mercy."

New dichotomy that touch on valid concepts, the typical understanding of these covenants, and the belief in their independent intent, advocates for a change in design, which disregards the supremacy of God's will. God is all-powerful, all-knowing, and ever-present; a principle of scripture that defies such a progressive, paradigmatic idealism. Nothing happens outside of God's will. In God's own words, "I am God, and there is none else; I am God, and there is none like me, declaring the end from the beginning.... My counsel shall stand, and I will do all my pleasure."[1]

While there is no denying that the Old and New Covenants each exist in their own right, and that they are unmistakably distinct in character, it nevertheless holds true that God declared the end from the beginning. The two primary covenants are not separate attempts at reconciliation, but interdependent and symbiotic covenants, both working together to accomplish the same end goal. God's singular plan incorporates both in tandem, and does so very deliberately. As will be discussed throughout this work, neither covenant can function alone.

Thus, relative to the supremacy of God's will, the periods of unique administration or forms of government — dispensations by definition — have no actual bearing or effect on the structure or integrity of God's plan, apart from that which he intended. Nothing concerning God's preordained will has changed, no matter the wickedness of man. Adam didn't ruin anything. He couldn't have ruined God's plan if he tried. Neither has a thousand generations of sinners interfered with God's plan. God will do all his pleasure.

---

1. Isa. 46:9-10.

Everything that has happened has been to the point and purpose of unveiling the mystery of the lamb, slain from the foundation of the world. Far from ruining that intended end result, every perceivable dispensation throughout the Bible has led to it.[1] Jesus Christ was always the objective.[2]

Nevertheless, the dispensational view thrives in mainstream Christianity, alleging a hindrance and alteration to God's plan via the agency of human corruption.

Church dogma is funny like that. Once we're taught something, it's difficult to see it any other way, and not everyone takes the time to investigate the deeper understandings of scripture. We are programmed with a certain bias, whether it be according to our denomination, the instruction of our minister or a trusted mentor, or even by our own studies which can sometimes be incomplete or misguided.

The bottom line is that the average Christian typically just doesn't know to believe anything different. They're taught what they're taught, and the greater majority take it at face value. They read their Bibles or daily devotions. They go to Bible study and read select sections of scripture that reinforce what they've been told. And so they continue on, believing in this crazy idea that man was able to defy the will of the all-powerful God of heaven and earth, thereby corrupting his perfect plan — while simultaneously maintaining that the will of God will be done. I dare say that it's somewhat comical. You can't fight the will of God. He will do all his pleasure ... unless we're talking about Adam eating from the tree and spoiling all of God's plans.

---

1. Rev. 13:8.
2. Gal. 3:16-18.

This duplicitous mentality, maintained even in systematic theology, results in two distinct philosophies on the subject.[1] On the one hand, the thinkers are inclined to believe that man did *not* go against God's will, but that he was acting within it. This theological idea is part of the doctrine of divine providence, sometimes referred to as the Divine Decree, whereby all things happen according to God's will, whether directly controlled or passively permitted.[2] In which case, the suggestion is that man fell through the approbation of God's permissive will. Being unable to directly compel man to sin without having some responsibility for the act, God simply orchestrated events to guarantee its certainty. He then turned a blind eye and permitted it to happen so his will would be accomplished.[3]

On the other hand, most Christians, regardless of denominational upbringing, instinctively reject the idea that the fall was God's will, or that he had any hand in it whatsoever. Let no man say when he is tempted that he is tempted of God.[4] Although we believe that God knows everything, and that nothing happens outside of God's will, a part of us still maintains a vague, idealistic conceptualization of the

---

1. Berkhof, *Systematic Theology*, 105, 222. Berkhof writes, "By his decree God rendered the sinful actions of man infallibly certain […]." Then, speaking of the original sin, he writes, "The essence of that sin lay in the fact that Adam placed himself in opposition to God, that he refused to subject his will to the will of God." In other words, Berkhof is saying that man had no choice but to defy God's will, though God's will was for man to defy him, rendering his defiance compliance. The notion is incongruous with itself.

2. Berkhof, *Systematic Theology*, 100-102, 165-169.

3. Berkhof, *Systematic Theology*, 105, 108.

4. Jas. 1:13.

whole affair somewhere in the back of our mind, where man ate from the tree completely against God's will while God was busy taking a bath or something. And boy was he mad when he found out!

For most, this is usually enough, even if it defies what we know about the power of God. They take it on faith that he had nothing to do with the fall, and they are no more interested in trying to figure out the particulars of the glaring inconsistencies than they are in trying to articulate them.

For the knowledge-seekers who ask the difficult questions, the scriptural reality is that God was there.[1] He knew what was happening, and he absolutely had the power to stop it. These facts lead them to the difficult and uncomfortable conclusion that the fall must have been God's will, else it wouldn't have happened.

When God didn't want Balaam to curse the Israelites, his curses came out as blessings.[2] When God wanted Jonah to go to Nineveh, he sent a tempest and a large fish to swallow him.[3] But while God has intervened in many things throughout the ages, he chose not to intervene here. He could have warded the tree of the knowledge of good and evil with thorns and thistle, or set his angels to guard it, as he did with the tree of life.[4] He could have hidden it. He could have left the tree out of the garden altogether, seeing that he's the one who put it there to begin with.[5] But he didn't. Man was

---

1. Jer. 23:24; Ps. 139:7-10; Job 34:21; Prov. 15:3.
2. Num. 22:1-24:25.
3. Jon. 1:1-3:3.
4. Gen. 3:23.
5. Gen. 2:9.

clearly permitted to fall.

I remember discussing this issue with a friend of mine over lunch at a local pizzeria one afternoon. In the face of facts, neither of us could dismiss the logical conclusion that it had to be God's will, and we agreed at the time that the fall, however seemingly callous it appeared to us, must have been willed as part of God's plan to demonstrate the glory of his mercy. My friend, in fact, dubbed the concept "mercy glory" as a means to reconcile ourselves with the idea that God actually willed man to fall.

However, the thought that God wanted or willed man to sin and die never sat well with me, and I'm sure that most Christians would agree with that sentiment. Sin and death were not, are not, and never will be his desire.[1] The Bible teaches that God is love, and that he wants none to perish.[2] He wants all to be saved and come to repentance and the knowledge of the truth.[3] Most of us would also agree that God would never make man sin, directly or indirectly. Responsibility for sin is entirely on us according to our own decisions.[4] Neither would God orchestrate a circumstance where sin was unavoidable. In the first place, he will not allow us to be tempted beyond what we are able to endure.[5] In the second place, deliberately causing a thing to happen is

---

1. Ezek. 18:23, 32, 33:11.

2. 1 Jn. 4:8, 16.

3. 2 Pet. 3:9; 1 Tim. 2:4.

4. Isa. 50:1. God here charges Israel with direct responsibility for her own bondage and divorcement as a result of her transgressions and iniquities. See also Isa. 30:1 and Ezek. 18:13, 20, 31.

5. 1 Cor. 10:13.

no different than doing it yourself. Christ made it clear that intent is equivalent to the act.[1] David put Uriah in harm's way on the front lines at Rabbah, believing he would be killed, and with the intent to effectuate it.[2] According to the prophet Nathan, this made David guilty of murder, though David himself did not physically wield the sword.[3] He slew Uriah "with the sword of the children of Ammon."

In light of God's character, his desires for righteousness, and his hatred of sin, it's ridiculous to conclude that God's will was for Adam to commit sin and die. It's even more ridiculous to believe that God controlled Adam's actions, overtly or covertly, or did anything to guarantee the certainty of the original sin.[4] This would make God guilty of the transgression, however clever the argument to the contrary.

Relative to the broader collection of scriptural facts, it's clear that the fall was not God's will. Rather, God's will was that man should have a choice, and that he should decide for himself whether he fell or not. Allowing Adam to sin was the unfortunate consequence God had to bear in surrendering his own sovereign will to the freedom of man's choice. For

---

1. Matt. 5:27-28.
2. 2 Sam. 11:14-15.
3. 2 Sam. 12:9; Berkhof, *Systematic Theology*, 108. This scriptural principle rules out the notion that God, for holy reasons or otherwise, "renders ... sinful acts certain," as Berkhof suggests. With the Law being holy, just and good, it is a contradiction to say that God would behave contrary to his own law in effectuating sin.
4. Berkhof, *Systematic Theology*, 105. Berkhof here describes sin as a certainty orchestrated by God, but without any interference of the finite will; viz. all of man's finite choices are irrelevant in the vacuum of God's intent to see him sin and fall.

good or ill, God so greatly esteemed that free will choice that he preferred to stand by while man destroyed himself, rather than compel him to serve mindlessly.

Understanding it in this way clarifies two issues at once. Any and all responsibility for Adam's sin belongs to Adam alone, not God, and the errant notion that man managed to resist the will of God, or defy it without God's knowledge, are eliminated. The moment man exercised his free will and made a *choice*, God's will was accomplished.

Then as now, life and death were placed before mankind, and it has always been up to man to choose, which is the very definition of free will.[1] God wants us to choose him, and to choose righteousness.[2] He doesn't want empty worship.[3] He wants our voluntary love.[4] We all have a choice in what we do, and to be judged accordingly.[5]

However, the point I'm making here is that the fall of man was not an anomalistic happenstance. Whether one holds to a more Calvinistic approach of divine providence or an Arminian view of God's foreknowledge of our freewill choices, the end result is the same.[6] God's plan, by design or

---

1. Deut. 30:19; Josh. 24:15, etc.
2. Deut. 7:7-11, 30:18-20.
3. Isa. 29:13; Matt. 15:8-9.
4. 1 Jn. 4:7-21.
5. Eccl. 12:14; Rom. 2:16.
6. John Calvin believed in predestination and preordination, meaning that God controls every aspect of our lives, except in matters of our finite decisions that have no bearing on the broader aspect of his will. Jacobus Arminius was on the opposite end of the theological spectrum in believing that we have absolute freewill, and that God renders his decisions based upon his foreknowledge of

foresight, took the fall of man into account.[1]

Ergo, the Bible doesn't teach us that man ruined God's plan. Nor does it teach us that God instituted failed attempt after failed attempt to reconcile us to himself. God's plan incorporated our sin. It was *because* man was going to sin that God's plan from the beginning was redemption. Christ was not a tragic remedy to a plan gone awry. He was the culmination of a plan that existed before the foundations of the world were laid.

> That it might be fulfilled which was spoken by the prophet, saying, I will open my mouth in parables; I will utter things which have been kept secret *from the foundation of the world.*[2]
>
> Come, ye blessed of my Father, inherit the kingdom prepared for you *from the foundation of the world.*[3]
>
> Now to him that is of power to stablish you according to my gospel, and the preaching of Jesus Christ, according to the revelation of the mystery, which was kept secret *since the world began.*[4]

---

our decisions. Further information is readily available with a bit of independent research as you so desire.

1. Num. 22:18, 38; Rom. 8:29-30. These two sections of scripture demonstrate the opposing views. In the one instance, there is a demonstration of free will being hindered by the will of God. In the other instance, there is evidence of his actions concerning individuals being governed by his foreknowledge.
2. Matt. 13:35.
3. Matt. 25:34.
4. Rom. 16:25.

But we speak the wisdom of God in a mystery, even the hidden wisdom, which God ordained *before the world* unto our glory.[1]

According as he hath chosen us in him *before the foundation of the world*, that we should be holy and without blame before him in love.[2]

And to make all men see what is the fellowship of the mystery, which *from the beginning of the world* hath been hid in God, who created all things by Jesus Christ.[3]

Even the mystery *which hath been hid from ages and from generations*, but now is made manifest to his saints.[4]

Who hath saved us, and called us with an holy calling, not according to our works, but according to his own purpose and grace, which was given us in Christ Jesus *before the world began*.[5]

[...] although the works were finished *from the foundation of the world*.[6]

[...] with the precious blood of Christ, as of a lamb without blemish and without spot: Who verily was foreordained *before the foundation of the world*, but was manifest in these

---

1. 1 Cor. 2:7.
2. Eph. 1:4.
3. Eph. 3:9.
4. Col. 1:26.
5. 2 Tim. 1:9.
6. Heb. 4:3.

last times for you.[1]

And all that dwell upon the earth shall worship him, whose names are not written in the book of life of the Lamb slain *from the foundation of the world*.[2]

Acceptance of this reality, of a fixed and deliberate plan versus a causal one, changes many of the dynamics of long held mainstream beliefs. We have to become like children and unlearn, at least for the moment, all that we think we know, and see the big picture.

The promise given to Abraham is the foundation, or preamble, of the New Covenant. Our faith in Christ merely brought that promise to fulfillment.[3] Because of the promise, the children of Israel were spared when Moses pleaded on their behalf.[4] Because of the promise, the branch of Jesse and the line of David were promised forevermore a son to sit upon the throne.[5] Even the law, Paul says, cannot disannul the promise.[6]

As G. Vos noted:

> It is clear from subsequent places how Scripture regards the Sinaitic covenant as a continuation of the covenant with Abraham: Exod 2:24, "And God remembered His covenant with Abraham, Isaac, and Jacob"; Leviticus 26:42, "Then I

---

1. 1 Pet. 1:19-20.
2. Rev. 13:8.
3. Gal. 3:22.
4. Deut. 9:24-29.
5. Jer. 33:14-17.
6. Gal. 3:17.

will remember my covenant with Jacob, with Isaac, with Abraham" (Deut 4:31; 2 Kgs 13:23). Again and again, there is a continual pointing back to the covenant with Abraham to show that the children of Israel were in that covenant.[1]

Dismissing, then, the dispensational myth, understand that everything falls beneath the parent umbrella of the promise made to Abraham, which was itself merely the first utterance of the plan that existed from the beginning. The Old and New Covenants alike are both subordinate to it.

In short, God saw the history of things to come. He saw the man he would create and the choice that would condemn him. He knew that through the knowledge of good and evil, mankind would become sinners.[2] Nevertheless, God determined at the dawn of creation that, for the sake of those he foreknew would choose him, his son should die so they could be gathered together in him, and so that those who trust in Christ would bring glory to the grace of God.[3] The promise was made to Abraham, and the crucifixion and resurrection brought it to fruition, fulfilling God's plan of redemption for the sin he knew man would commit before Adam drew his first breath.

Jesus truly is the alpha and the omega, the beginning and end of all things.[4] By him were all things made, and through

---

1. Geerhardus Vos, *Reformed Dogmatics*, vol. 2, *Anthropology*, trans. and ed. Richard B. Gaffin Jr. (Bellingham, WA: Lexham Press, 2012-14), 133.

2. Rom. 5:12-14.

3. Rom. 8:29; Eph. 1:4-12; 1 Pet. 1:18-21.

4. Rev. 1:8, 11, 17.

him are all things gathered together unto God.[1] While there have been many covenants, and perhaps even many unique periods of administration, there has only ever been one plan. That plan was Jesus Christ, and it never changed.

> Having made known unto us the mystery of his will, according to his good pleasure which he hath purposed in himself: That in the dispensation of the fullness of times he might gather together in one all things in Christ, both which are in heaven, and which are on earth; *even* in him: In whom also we have obtained an inheritance, being predestinated according to the purpose of him who worketh all things after the counsel of his own will.[2]

> For whom he did foreknow, he also did predestinate *to be* conformed to the image of his Son, that he might be the firstborn among many brethren. Moreover whom he did predestinate, them he also called: and whom he called, them he also justified: and whom he justified, them he also glorified.[3]

---

1. Jn. 1:3; Col. 1:16-17; Eph. 1:9-11.
2. Eph. 1:9-11.
3. Rom. 8:29-30.

2

The Law

So the next question is, if the plan has always been Jesus Christ, and nothing can supersede it, why did the Old Covenant even exist? Why did God go from the promise to Abraham, then to the Old Covenant, only to bring us right back to the promise with a New Covenant? Why bother with the Law at all? If it can't supersede Christ, who was both before and after, *what's the point*? What purpose does it serve?

To this there are so many answers, a comprehensive list would be impossible to give. God's goals and objectives are as complex as the law itself, and no one can truly know every facet of God's mind.[1] However, Paul, after extolling the virtues of faith and expounding on the inadequacies of the law as a redeeming covenant, asks, rhetorically, the very same question, and in the same context. "And this I say, that the covenant, that was confirmed before of God in Christ, the law, which was four hundred and thirty years after, cannot disannul, that it should make the promise of none effect. [...]

---

1. Isa. 55:8-9.

The Law

Wherefore then serveth the law?"[1]

To this question he answers rather succinctly, "It was added because of transgressions," to which many concepts and statements throughout the course of his letters testify to one degree or another.[2] The law, in short, was added because of sin, and even more broadly, because of sinfulness.

The law, for example, due to our sinful natures, taught us how to be righteous, how to judge righteously, and generally speaking, how to treat our neighbors justly and with respect. We may have had the knowledge of good and evil, but we clearly needed to be instructed in choosing the one and rejecting the other.[3] This is evident enough in the fact that we needed a law to tell us not to trip blind people.[4] Laws that random don't exist without a precedent. If such a law was given, it means that someone, or many someones, actually did such a thing. They had obviously not grasped the concept of common sense and decency. Nor has mankind's behavior over the centuries demonstrated any significant improvement.

The fact is, despite our general sense of right and wrong, we tend to talk ourselves into doing what we want to do rather than what we should do, and then justify or rationalize the deed. This has always been so.[5] Our desire is for sin.[6] And in the absence of law, justification for wrong-doing is

---

1. Gal. 3:17-19.
2. Gal. 3:19.
3. Deut. 1:39; Isa. 7:15-16.
4. Lev. 19:14.
5. Isa. 30:1, 55:8-9.
6. Gen. 4:7.

easily feigned, even to ourselves.

To remedy the situation, God gave mankind the written law and took the guess work out of the equation.[1] This is right. That is wrong. Whatever justification you've concocted in your mind, if it says, "don't do it," then don't do it. It's wrong. It's all very black and white.

The law is therefore a definitive guide, separating right from wrong.[2] If we sin, it's because we're ignoring the rules, not because we don't know them.

In another explanation, Paul tells us that the law was our schoolmaster, which is just an archaic way of saying it was our guardian, from the same derivative word from which we get *agōgē*, a Greek school of training where the young were trained in the lifestyle chosen for them by the state.[3] The law exercised a general supervision over our moral and physical well-being, teaching us, shaping us, and molding us in preparation for adult citizenship in the kingdom of God. We were its ward.[4]

In the truest sense of the word used, imagine the law as a boarding school, complete with its rules, regulations, and curriculum. Our life before going to the university is immature, undisciplined, and ignorant, and perhaps even a bit chaotic. Our life after the university is mature, refined, knowledgeable, and wise. But our time *at* the university is strictly regimented, to shape the way we think and behave, to educate us, discipline us, and to prepare us for life outside the

---

1. Ezek. 20:11.
2. Deut. 30:15, 19.
3. Gal. 3:24. The Greek word here is παιδαγωγός.
4. Gal. 3:24.

university walls. Its governance ensures that we are fully equipped when it is time to leave its care and enter into the freedom of the promise.[1]

It should be further recognized that the concept in Paul's description of the law's power over us in this instance, and its subsequent dissolution with the fulfillment of the promise, demonstrates also its transient authority, which is an important point worthy of later note. The law was not a permanent institution, and it was never meant to be. It was, in this explanation, an institution of refinement, and at least moderately in line with the early church's position on a dispensational trichotomy; namely *ante legem*, *sub lege* and *post legem*, referring to the separate periods of administration before, during, and after the law.[2]

In a third, and very prominently expounded principle, Paul expresses in great detail how the law serves to eliminate all excuses and denial of wrongdoing. As I already pointed out, we have a bad habit of pushing down our conscience and justifying our sin.[3] I'm sure I'm not the only one out there who has done, or thought to do, something I knew I shouldn't, only to feel an immediate surge of conviction. The law has the power to convict, accuse, and to condemn, because the knowledge of the law undeniably and definitively quantifies sin.[4] There are no shades of gray. While we might attempt to justify our actions in the absence of a governing

---

1. Gal. 3:23-29, 4:1-5.
2. Geerhardus Vos, *Reformed Dogmatics*, vol. 2, *Anthropology*, trans. and ed. Richard B. Gaffin Jr. (Bellingham, WA: Lexham Press, 2012-14), 133.
3. Rom. 3:19-20.
4. 4 Jn. 5:45, 8:9; 2 Cor. 3:6-11; Rom. 3:20.

law, the existence of the law holds us accountable.[1]

And to clarify, this doesn't mean that the law is required for sin to exist, which I've heard advocated on more than one occasion. While Paul says that where there is no law, there is no transgression, he also clearly tells us that sin was in the world well in advance of the law.[2] We can readily see by the example of Cain that sin laid in wait if he did not do rightly, and James later tells us that if anyone knows to do a good thing and does not do it, to him it is sin, demonstrating that sin existed prior to the law, and exists still beyond the advent of Christ.[3]

Paul's statements, taken in the greater context, very plainly impart the message that the law doesn't create the sin. It merely exposes the sin for what it is, so that "sin might appear sin, and by the commandment become exceedingly sinful."[4] It identifies the sin in a legal and formal way, and convicts us of our transgressions.[5] It takes away all excuses, and provides God a clear and justifiable precedent to impute our transgressions and find the world guilty.[6]

The law, in short, is an instrument of accusation.[7]

And so, as it concerns the law being added because of sin, we can see in these most fundamental elements that the law taught us the difference between right and wrong. It

---

1. Rom. 5:13-14, 4:15.
2. Rom. 4:15, 5:13.
3. Gen. 4:7; Jas. 4:17.
4. Rom. 7:13, 5:20.
5. Rom. 2:14-15.
6. Rom. 3:19.
7. Jn. 5:45.

strictly governed our lives and taught us how to behave rightly. And it dispensed righteous justice for our sin. Concerning these points, most, I'm certain, would readily agree.

But it's important to recognize that there are other, less conspicuous purposes to the law, which are directly relevant to the topic at hand.

Foremost of the inherent objectives of the law, although often poorly understood by mainstream Christians, is to provide us some succor against an otherwise binding declaration. That is to say, God declared that man would die if he ate from the tree of the knowledge of good and evil, and since man ate from the tree, man had to die. God's declaration made no allowance for redemption.

God did not say, "in the day that thou eatest thereof thou shalt surely die … *unless*" or "*until* …" He said that "in the day that thou eatest thereof thou shalt surely die," period.[1]

As a result, death, as Paul says, reigned from Adam to Moses, because no ready means existed to reverse the death man brought upon himself. Sin had entered into the world and spread to each successive generation by the knowledge of good and evil. It infected the world with the aftermath of what we call the original sin, by which each of us has sinned according to our knowledge of right and wrong and become, by definition, sinners. And so death passed upon us all.[2]

---

1. Gen. 2:17.
2. Rom. 5:12-14, 19. It is worth noting that Paul does not say that through Adam we all have sin, but that through him, sin entered the world, and all have sinned as a result. The original sin is a specific instance of behavior that resulted in the ability to sin through the knowledge of good and evil, making us all "sinners." But just as a singer is a person who sings, a sinner is a person who sins. The brand of "sinner" defines what we are, not what we have. And so the

If not for the law, there would have been no hope, just as the Gentiles had no hope prior to Christ, being strangers to the covenants of promise.[1] They were separated by the enmity put between the woman's seed and the serpent's, and made aliens to the commonwealth of Israel.[2] It was Christ who abolished that enmity, and broke down the middle wall of partition between Jew and Gentile, making the two people one.[3]

That enmity was the Law of Moses. And just as the Gentiles had no hope without it, so should it be rightly inferred that no one else had hope without it.[4] It's not a coincidence that Paul specified the period from Adam to Moses, and not the period from Adam to Abraham, which is when the promise was given. The fact is, life wasn't possible for sinners before the law. The receiving of the law was the defining

---

consequences of the original sin has therefore passed through the generations by definable acts of sin, as opposed to the idea that we all contracted sin at birth like a spiritual virus. Our sins are not inherited, but committed. The very notion of inherited sin is admonished by God himself. The son does not bear the iniquity of the father (Ezek. 18:1-20).

1. Eph. 2:12.
2. Gen. 3:15; Eph. 2:12. The parallel here is undeniable. In both Genesis and Ephesians, there are two groups represented. In both instances, they are separated by the enmity. The Gentiles were clearly given over to the devil, since they were without God and without hope, whereas the Jews were the chosen people of God. And so the removal of the enmity eliminated the separation between the two seeds and made them one people. And the only thing separating Jew and Gentile was the law, which provided the Jews a commonwealth and a covenant of promise, while simultaneously denying the Gentiles the same. Thus, the enmity in Eph. 2:12 is clearly that of Gen. 3:15, despite any elaborate theology concerning Christ surrounding the Genesis passage.
3. Eph. 2:14-15; Rom. 11:13-27. Cf. Rom. 9:25; Hos. 2:23.
4. Eph. 2:14-15.

The Law | 23

moment that changed our fates. During the period from Adam to Moses, Jew and Gentile alike were denied the benefit of the forthcoming promise not yet delivered, and they were dead in their sins because the law had not yet been given. For all living souls, there was only the declaration of death, with no provision for redemption. Even the tree of life was deliberately withheld, warded and protected by God so we wouldn't live forever in defiance of his decree.

> And the Lord God said, Behold, the man is become as one of us, to know good and evil: and now, lest he put forth his hand, and take also of the tree of life, and eat, and live forever: therefore the Lord God sent him forth from the garden of Eden, to till the ground from whence he was taken. So he drove out the man; and he placed at the east of the garden of Eden Cherubims, and a flaming sword which turned every way, to keep the way of the tree of life.[1]

But to reiterate the point from chapter one, God was not ignorant of what was going to happen, whether as a matter of providence or foreknowledge. His plan preexisted mankind. While man may have been permitted to sin and fall, it was never God's *desire* that either should happen.[2] So the law became our avenue for life through obedience, while simultaneously providing us the provisionary loophole his original declaration lacked, knowing that in this, too, we would inevitably fail.[3] A loophole, I might add, that did not

---

1. Gen. 3:22-24.
2. Ezek. 18:32, 33:11; Lam. 3:33-42; 2 Pet. 3:9.
3. Deut. 4:1-3, 5:33, 8:1, 16:20, 30:6.

depend upon us, but upon him, just as Paul declares concerning the gift of salvation. It rests not upon our own righteousness or justification, but on that of Christ.[1]

The law is at once the source of our salvation and condemnation, our life and our death, and being amongst the least understood institutions God has ever given us, it has proven to be one of the greatest Biblical ironies. As Paul tells us, "if there had been a law given which could have given life, verily righteousness should have been by the law."[2] And yet, the law *does* provide us both life and righteousness, which is precisely why it was given. It just doesn't provide it to sinners according to their conduct or obedience, but according to the fine print, by means of substitutiary atonement. It allowed Christ to die in our place.

And even in this, the subtlety of the law's many purposes comes to light. Relative to substitutiary atonement, the law provides a formal indictment of infractions to facilitate the legitimate transference of our sins. For God to save the world through Christ, it was necessary to formally and legally condemn it according to lawfully defined transgressions. You can't sell a car without a title showing the vehicle details and proof of ownership. Before Christ could bear our sins, God first had to identify them, and demonstrate our culpability.

Furthermore, the process of our necessary condemnation is yet another subtle nuance that goes unnoticed. There is a definable difference between death and condemnation. The world was spiritually dead prior to the law, including

---

[1]. Rom. 3:25-28; Eph. 2:8; Tit. 3:3-7.
[2]. Gal. 3:21.

The Law | 25

patriarchs like Noah and Abraham. Condemnation, on the other hand, is a legalistic sentence resulting from trial and litigation, which none were afforded in the absence of the law.[1] While Adam's sin may have been clearly defined by the commandment he was given in the garden, the rest of us, whose sins were not "after the similitude of Adam's transgression," and therefore not according to any stated law, remained unindicted and without the benefit of a proper accusation or trial. Sin is not imputed where there is no law.[2] The law therefore entered that sin might abound, and that it would be revealed as the sin it is, bringing about a universal condemnation *ab initio*, imputing and accusing the sin of sinners from Adam forward, with death forestalled until Judgement.[3] By the law, we are condemned to die rather than just being dead. And condemnation, being legal in nature, allows for the possibility of clemency, and in the case of the law of Moses specifically, propitiation. While there's life, there's hope.[4] Independently, the law was ultimately imperfect as a covenant of salvation due to man's weakness.[5] But it served the purpose of affording God the legal precedent to give

---

1. 1 Cor. 15:22; Rom. 5:12-14.
2. Rom. 5:12-14, 2:11-15, 3:23.
3. 1 Cor. 15:22; Rom. 5:12-14, 20, 14:10; 2 Tim. 4:1; Rev. 11;18, 20:12. Paul is saying that the sin during the pre-law period was imputed retroactively with the introduction of the law. All those prior to the law would be otherwise lost, including Noah, Abraham, Isaac, Jacob, Joseph, Judah, and the patriarchs of the other ten tribes, and many other notable and faithful followers of God.
4. Eccl. 9:4.
5. Heb. 7:18, 8:6-8.

mankind the hope of life, whereas such did not formerly exist beneath the shadow of his declaration.[1] And so with our condemnation comes a new hope of life in the face of certain death.

So wherefore then serveth the law? As already stated, there are many purposes. The law was, in part, to define right and wrong. It was, in part, our guardian, to mold, discipline, and educate us in righteousness until the appointed time when the promise would be fulfilled and the law would be put into our hearts and minds.[2] And it was, in part, to expose and define sin so the world would be without excuse.

But most importantly, it was given in order to save us.

As already discussed, Christ was the plan from the beginning. The law was just the next phase. God's declaration in the garden didn't go away. His word is absolute, because God can't lie.[3] It is not a coincidence that Jesus referred to himself as the son of man.[4] Man had to pay the price for the transgression in the garden. The law merely transferred the penalty to Jesus Christ, God as man, made of a woman, made under the law, to redeem them that were under the law.[5] When he died as a ransom for the world, God's irreversible

---

1. Heb. 7:19; Rom. 8:3-4.
2. Heb. 8:8-10; Jer. 31:31-33.
3. Heb. 6:16-18.
4. Adam and man, or mankind, are interchangeable in Hebrew (אָדָם). The context decides the application, whether the word refers to Adam, the individual, as a proper name, or whether it refers to mankind in general. When Jesus calls himself the son of man, his reference is to mankind (ἄνθρωπος), just as the Hebrew predominantly uses אָדָם when speaking of mankind generally, and only thirteen times as a proper name.
5. Jn. 1:1, 14; Gal. 4:4-5.

declaration of death in the Garden of Eden, rather than being abrogated, was satisfied and fulfilled. The price of death was paid.[1]

---

1. Matt. 20:28; Mk. 10:45; 1 Tim. 2:6; 1 Cor. 6:20, 7:23.

3

The Oath

But although I have hopefully explained the law's purpose to you adequately, it is still needful to impart to you an understanding of its implementation, its ratification, and the nature of our specific connection to it, which is integral to the salvation process. No one is automatically obligated to the covenantal law. It has to be voluntarily entered into. In fact, our acknowledgement and acceptance of our subjectivity to the law is the very thing that makes the confession of our sins a necessity to salvation.[1] It is a concession to the authority of the law that defines the sin. And only by the law and its authority are we able to profit by the covenant's particulars, whereas a rejection of the law and its salvific authority renders it impotent in this regard.

This doesn't mean that the law is powerless to convict sinners if they reject its authority. To the contrary, the scriptures are clear that "what things soever the law saith, it saith to them who are under the law: that every mouth may be

---

1. 1 Jn 1:8-9.

stopped, and all the world may become guilty before God."[1] The law condemns "all the world," despite individual acceptance or rejection.

However, just as Christ's death has no benefit to someone who does not believe he is the son of God, neither does the law benefit someone who rejects its authority. Those who have it and accept it are judged by it. But having accepted it, they are also able to receive the promises and benefits it affords. Those who do not have it, or do not accept it, become a law unto themselves.[2] While their awareness of wrongdoing leaves them equally guilty before God, their self-conceived law of conscience differs from the law proper in that it carries no authority of redemption. God's ability to substitute Christ in our place is a benefit exclusive to the constitution of the covenantal law, whereas the law of conscience offers no such provision. The bare notions of right and wrong merely convict us. Outside of the covenantal legal structure, advocacy doesn't exist. Christ is of no benefit.

Therefore, to reject the covenantal law is to be separated from all hope and promise of salvation. As noted in the previous chapter, Gentiles were excluded from the citizenship of Israel. They were separate from the seed of Abraham and the associated promise. Thus, those outside of the law are not God's people. They are strangers to the covenants of promise, devoid of any hope, and ultimately without God.[3] Outside of the covenants, we are separated from him.

---

1. Rom. 3:19.
2. Rom. 2:11-15.
3. Eph. 2:12.

But by faith we become citizens of Israel, and by extension the descendants of Abraham's seed. We are all one in Christ, and as such, heirs to the promise.[1] Contrary to the ideas of Replacement Theology, which teaches that Christians took the place of Jews, believers actually *become* Jews, and partakers of both the Abrahamic and the Mosaic covenants. This is at the heart of one of Paul's arguments.

> For he is not a Jew, which is one outwardly; neither is that circumcision, which is outward in the flesh: But he is a Jew, which is one inwardly; and circumcision is that of the heart, in the spirit, and not in the letter; whose praise is not of men, but of God.[2]

The Gentile, being a wild olive branch, has been grafted into the good olive tree by faith, making us no longer aliens to the commonwealth of Israel, or strangers to the covenants of promise, but citizens in the community of God.[3]

---

1. Gal. 3:16, 26-28.
2. Rom. 2:28-29. Cf. Col. 2:11; Deut. 10:16-17, 30:6.
3. Rom. 11:16-32. Confusion on this topic frequently leads to erroneous ideas, such as Replacement Theology, which alleges that Christians took the place of the Jews, based primarily on Matt. 21:43. However, Jesus' statement speaks more to authority, since the priests in charge were not bearing the fruits of the kingdom of God. Politically, culturally and authoritatively, another nation would be given charge of the kingdom of God, as history clearly demonstrates to have taken place. The Roman Catholic church had charge of the spread of Christianity and authority over the oracles of God for over a thousand years, where it had previously been in the sole charge of the Jewish authority (Rom. 3:2). But the Jews were still the chosen people of God. So contrary to the contentions of some, Christians have not replaced the Jews. Christians are Jews. It is not our birth, but our hearts and faith that makes us Jews.

Relative to this truth, understand that faith and legal inclusion are mutual aspects of the process. It is the law that makes Christ's substitution possible. To benefit from his atoning sacrifice, we have to first be subject to the covenant that empowers it. And so by faith we become part of the nation of Israel, and as Israel we are obligated to the covenant made at Sinai, whereby faith becomes the facilitating instrument in subjecting us to the existing covenant of the law.

In other words, the moment you accepted Christ, you became a Jew in spirit, circumcised in heart, and were included by default through faith into the covenant of the law. While some might be prematurely inclined to criticize this particular detail, it is something that should not be overlooked. Jesus said that he was not sent except to the lost sheep of the house of Israel.[1] This now includes you. Salvation, he said, is of the Jews.[2] This, too, now includes you. God declared that when he made the new covenant — *with the house of Israel, and with the house of Judah* — Israel was to receive mercy, while those who in former times were not his people were to receive inclusion and *become* his people, and he their God.[3]

So by faith we have become Jews, and have been received into the covenants of promise.

> Wherefore remember, that ye being in time past Gentiles in the flesh, ... without Christ, being aliens from the commonwealth of Israel, and strangers from the covenants of promise,

---

1. Matt. 15:24.
2. Jn. 4:22.
3. Hos. 2:23, 1:10; Jer. 31:31-33; Rom. 9:25-26.

having no hope, and without God in the world: But now in Christ Jesus ye who sometimes were far off are made nigh by the blood of Christ.... For through him we both have access by one Spirit unto the Father. Now therefore ye are no more strangers and foreigners, but fellow citizens with the saints, and of the household of God; And are built upon the foundation of the apostles and prophets, Jesus Christ himself being the chief corner stone; In whom all the building fitly framed together groweth unto an holy temple in the Lord: In whom ye also are builded together for an habitation of God through the Spirit.[1]

But to step back to the original thought, we have a connection to the Old Covenant that goes beyond the virtue of its conception, meaning that we are not bound to it just because it exists.[2] It is an agreement that had to be entered into voluntarily by both God and man at the time of its establishment. We both have commitments to each other as part of the agreement, as we both have benefits to be derived from it. Furthermore, we are both formally obligated to it. As Christ says, "Till heaven and earth pass, one jot or one tittle shall in no wise pass from the law, till all be fulfilled."[3]

Paul describes the bond in one instance as being similar to the relationship between a master and servant; servitude in perpetuity.[4] In another explanation, which I find to be even

---

1. Eph. 2:11-13, 2:18-22.
2. Rom. 4:6-8.
3. Matt. 5:18.
4. Rom. 6:16-23.

more to the point, our bond to the law is compared to a marriage.[1] In both illustrations — and this is especially key — the law has legal authority over us. It is a binding authority that obligates us to certain behavior by a legal precedent.

God didn't merely say, "do this," or "do that," and just like that we were bound. The covenant of the law was a contractual offer. It essentially stated that if we kept certain commandments and statutes, he would give us life in exchange, with something not too dissimilar from a non-compliance clause that would condemn us to a state of death and curses if we didn't uphold our end of the bargain.[2] Assuming everyone kept to the terms of the contract, it was a win-win arrangement. God got righteous and obedient worshippers out of the deal. We got life, in spite of Adam's failing. All we had to do was keep the commandments and statutes.

However, while successive generations of Jews were "grandfathered" into the existing covenant, and believers continue to enter it by faith, certain legalities still needed to be observed at its foundation. Like any other contract, it had to be formally implemented at the time of its establishment, complete with a proverbial signature on the dotted line. As stated at the beginning of this chapter, it had to be ratified, or made legally binding, in order to have any authority to work to our advantage. In this particular case, it was consummated with the blood of animals, and confirmed by an oath of affirmation, complete with witnesses.[3]

---

1. Rom. 7:1-6.
2. Ezek. 18:1 et seq.; Deut. 30:19, 28:2-14, 15-45.
3. Heb. 9:15-22; Deut. 29:10-12, 14-15, 30:19.

> Ye stand this day all of you before the Lord your God […] that thou shouldest enter into covenant with the Lord thy God, and into his oath, which the Lord thy God maketh with thee this day.[1]
>
> I call heaven and earth to record this day against you, that I have set before you life and death, blessing and cursing: therefore, choose life, that both thou and thy seed may live.[2]
>
> Neither with you only do I make this covenant and this oath; but with him that standeth here with us this day before the Lord our God, and also with him that is not here with us this day.[3]

Like I said before, in many respects our relationship to the law is not unlike a marriage, as Paul very appropriately describes it. We are legally bound and obligated to it by an oath. It is, therefore, perpetually binding upon all who enter into it, and this fact plays a significant role later on, as will be discussed in the appropriate chapter.

Meanwhile, this oath-bound condition creates some interesting dynamics to the broader picture. As we can see in the case of Jephthah, though it should cost us our own children, God will require of us all that we have sworn.[4] The law states that "if a man vow a vow unto the Lord, or swear an oath to bind his soul with a bond, he shall not break his word.

---

1. Deut. 29:10-12.
2. Deut. 30:19.
3. Deut. 29:14-15.
4. Judg. 11:30-35. Jephthah swore to offer up in sacrifice the first thing that greeted him if God would grant him victory and a safe return. That first thing ended up being his own daughter.

The Oath

He shall do according to all that proceedeth out of his mouth."[1]

The absoluteness of this is further exemplified by a precise understanding of the nature of oaths in general. To swear an oath is to swear by the name of God, and to swear falsely by the name of God is a direct violation of the covenantal agreement made, for which God will not hold us guiltless. As Jesus clearly demonstrates, *all* oaths, no matter what we swear them on, are binding on our soul, because every oath, great or small, whether sworn on the lives of our children or sworn on the well-being of our grandmother's toaster, are sworn upon the surety of God himself.[2]

> Woe unto you, ye blind guides, which say, Whosoever shall swear by the temple, it is nothing; but whosoever shall swear by the gold of the temple, he is a debtor! Ye fools and blind: for whether is greater, the gold, or the temple that sanctifieth the gold? And, Whosoever shall swear by the altar, it is nothing; but whosoever sweareth by the gift that is upon it, he is guilty. Ye fools and blind: for whether is greater, the gift, or the altar that sanctifieth the gift? Whoso therefore shall swear by the altar, sweareth by it, and by all things thereon. And whoso shall swear by the temple, sweareth by it, and by him that dwelleth therein. And he that shall swear by heaven, sweareth by the throne of God, and by him that sitteth thereon.[3]

So, whether directly or by extension, having sworn on

---

1. Num. 30:2.
2. Matt. 23:16-22.
3. Matt. 23:16-22.

the name of God, the negative prohibition stands that we "shalt not take the name of the Lord thy God in vain."[1]

And for clarification, while most mistakenly identify this as a commandment to not use God's name as profanity, early Jewish sources actually demonstrate the historical understanding of this commandment to be an injunction against swearing falsely by the name of God. Although the use of God's name as profanity *is* prohibited, the two acts are not one and the same.[2]

The following demonstrate the understanding of the third commandment from an ancient perspective.

> *Josephus* — [...] The third [commandment], [is] that we must not swear by God in a false matter.[3]

> *Philo* — The next commandment is, "not to take the name of God in vain." [...] For an oath is the calling of God to give his testimony concerning the matters which are in doubt; and it is a most impious thing to invoke God to be witness to a lie.[4]

> *Talmud* — When R. Dimi came [from Palestine] he said that R. Johanan said: [...] [If one says: 'I swear] I have eaten' or, '[I swear] I have not eaten,' [and it was untrue,] it is a vain oath, and its prohibition is [derived] from this [verse]: Thou

---

1. Exod. 20:7.
2. Lev. 19:12; Joseph. *AJ* 3.91; Philo *De Dec.* 82-95; Talmud, *Shevu'oth* 20b; Lev. 19:12.
3. Joseph. *AJ* 3.91-92.
4. Philo, *De Dec.* 82-86.

shalt not take the name of the Lord thy God in vain.[1]

Therefore, recognize that all those who enter in beneath the covenant of the law are bound by an oath, sworn on the name of God. We can't rescind the oath. We can't void it. There is no way around it. And God will not hold us guiltless if, by not keeping the whole law, we should prove to have taken his name in vain.[2]

At the same time, there is a reciprocal counterpart to our oath. You have to remember that this covenant was entered into by *both* parties, and with the same sureties, meaning that we weren't the only ones to swear an oath, vowing to keep our part of the agreement. God, too, made an oath, swearing that he would punish his enemies, who are demonstrated in Daniel to be those who do not keep the commandments and statutes of the Lord.[3] God said to the children of Israel:

> See now that I, *even* I, *am* he, and *there is* no god with me: I kill, and I make alive; I wound, and I heal: neither *is there any* that can deliver out of my hand. For I lift up my hand to heaven, and say, I live for ever. If I whet my glittering sword, and mine hand take hold on judgment; I will render vengeance to mine enemies, and will reward them that hate me.[4]

---

1. Exod. 20:7; Talmud, *Shevu'oth* 20b.

2. Exod. 20:7.

3. Deut. 32:39-41, 28:45-68; Dan. 9:11. The curse, having been promised by oath in the law of Moses, is specifically spelled out by Daniel, saying, "Yea, all Israel have transgressed thy law, even by departing, that they might not obey thy voice; therefore the curse is poured upon us, and the oath that is written in the law of Moses the servant of God, because we have sinned against him."

4. Deut. 32:39-41. Cf. Judg. 2:15; Isa. 45:23; Jer. 44:26-29. While Deuteronomy

In this very dramatic instance, God swears an oath, directly invoking his own name. This same formula can be observed throughout the Old Testament by individuals swearing on the name of God, saying, "As the Lord lives….,"[1] Here, when God says, "I am God, and I live forever….," he is saying the same thing, but in the first person. He even makes the gesture of raising his hand to heaven as Abram does in Genesis.[2]

And so the two parts of the whole present us with a rather interesting scenario. Since all have sinned and fall short of the glory of God, everyone under the covenant of the law is guilty of being an oath-breaker.[3] As James tells us, to break one law is to be guilty of them all, and to be convinced of the law as a transgressor.[4] This is why it's an all or nothing situation, and why all sin is counted the same. It's not that murder and lying are on an even keel on the sin-severity scale. It's "keep it all" or "be guilty of it all" because to sin is to despise the oath and to break the covenant.[5]

Thus, we are confronted with a substantial difficulty. Having sworn on the name of God, he will not hold us guiltless.[6] Having taken an oath, he will require of us all that has

---

shows the invoking of the actual oath, these other examples demonstrate that it was, in fact, an oath.

1. Jer. 4:2, 5:2, 12:16. There are many other instances, but these examples thoroughly demonstrate the deliberate application of the phrase in swearing.
2. Gen. 14:22.
3. Ezek. 16:59, 17:16, 17:19.
4. Jas. 2:10-11; cf. Gal. 5:3.
5. Ezek. 16:59, 17:19.
6. Exod. 20:7.

proceeded out of our mouths.[1] And since God not only declared that he would not hold us guiltless, but swore by his own name that he would punish his enemies, he is oath-bound to punish us as a consequence of our breaking the covenant. God can't take his own name in vain any more than we can.

So to answer a question posed at the beginning of the book — why couldn't God simply say, "I forgive you," and let that be the end of it — it was because he was oath-bound to judge us. We swore an oath to obey. He swore an oath to punish us if we did not. His word is inviolate.

---

1. Num. 30:2.

4

The Relationship

Now, before we can discuss the solution to our condemnation difficulty, it is necessary to first elaborate on the nature of our relationship to God, which plays a direct role in the details of Christ's sacrifice. We have to set the stage for why his death accomplished what it did, which is the question this book is ultimately here to answer. Why does his death save us? And even more particularly, why did he have to die in order to accomplish it?

There are, of course, always the immediate, stock responses to these sorts of questions. The law demanded animal sacrifices for the forgiveness of sins, so Jesus is held to that standard, being himself the Lamb of God.[1] The shedding of blood was necessary, so he had to die as a sacrifice for the remission of sins.[2]

But these sorts of answers fall more into the category of "what" rather than "why." Sacrificing an animal was what

---

1. Lev. 5:5-6, et al.; Jn. 1:29.
2. Heb. 9:22.

you did, just as forgiveness was what it accomplished. But we are left sorely wanting for an explanation on why there had to be a sacrifice in the first place, or why that sacrifice forgave sins. The "whys" so commonly expressed in mainstream Christianity unilaterally boil down to the fiat of the law. Animal sacrifices were necessary, so far as most people are able to explain it, for no better reason than because the law said so. The blood of these sacrifices forgave sins, likewise, because the law said so. Even when they attempt to use the idea retroactively to examples in the prelaw period, they are still explanations biased by the examples found in the law; explanations they would have never contemplated except that the law teaches sacrifices for the remission of sins.

I've found the difficulty so many people have in answering the question, "why did he have to die," very reminiscent of a movie I once watched, where the father was explaining the fundamentals of baseball to his son. The kid, having never seen the game first hand, and knowing nothing about it besides the rules as his father taught them, just couldn't comprehend the idea of why the runner had to run the bases. Nor could his father adequately explain it to him. The best answer the father was able to give was, "because he *must!*"

While we keep hearing answers like, "we are saved because he died on the cross," or, "he had to die because the law demanded a sacrifice," or, "because he was the lamb of God," or, "there had to be the shedding of blood," etc., these answers are substantively equivalent to, "because he *must!*"

But an analogy more suited to our topic would be closer to talking about the functionality of a light switch. You need light, and to get it, you flip the switch. It's common knowledge. The words "on" and "off" are even stamped into the switch. But flipping the switch isn't what gives you light. It merely facilitates a process that, although dependent upon the switch, is far more complex. The switch completes the circuit that allows the electricity to be conducted to the bulb, which was itself carefully crafted to receive the electricity in a particular way to generate light.

Like the light switch, Christ's sacrifice was little more than a means of allowing the power behind salvation to flow through. While his death was an absolutely necessary element in the process, by itself it accomplished nothing. It was just one of many needful steps in the grand design of salvation.

God's relationship with us is what makes the sacrifice necessary and gives it its functional purpose. Nothing with God is arbitrary. God did not sit on his throne in heaven and say to himself, "I think I'll make them kill stuff for forgiveness." I think we would all agree that he is not so capricious. Every law and every sacrifice was a calculated, methodical, and *necessary* aspect in achieving the goal of redemption according to specific cause and effect realities. If the law said something had to die, it was because something had to die for the process to work. It was not, as I already said, a matter of arbitrary ordination. Christ died as the necessary effect of an existing cause, and to understand why his death was able to facilitate the desired end result, we must elaborate on the relationship. Without it, Christ's death is pointless.

Now, I should state for clarification that the relationship I am referring to is intrinsic to the covenant. When you enter into the New Covenant through faith, you likewise enter into the relationship with God. It is not a thing you do or a behavior that you adopt. It is a thing that simply is. The two go hand in hand. So the discussion here about our relationship with God should not be misunderstood to be of the "personal relationship" sort advocated by many Pentecostals, where you need to be speaking in tongues and basking in the anointing of the Holy Spirit, or waving your hands in the air. Our relationship with God is a bit more formal than that, and is in no way determined or dictated by our manner of worship. You do not have more of a relationship with God because you sing, dance, or speak in tongues, or because you embrace a more Charismatic, Pentecostal type of worship. Neither do you have a lesser relationship because you are a quiet bookworm who prefers to show his or her dedication through study, or because you prefer a more liturgical brand of worship, or "high church" worship as we like to call it here in the south. Our relationship with God is the same regardless.

We are the bride of Christ.

Our relationship with God is a marriage. And it is safe to say that most are at least aware of this Biblical concept, even if they have not fully explored it. The roots of God's particular relationship with his people goes all the way back to the Old Testament, where it is conspicuously designated a marriage in more than one instance.[1] In fact, the "marriage" language used in the Old Testament is so plain and deliberate that God even goes so far as to give Israel a bill of divorce and "put her away" for her many adulteries.[2] His anger and

---

1. Isa. 54:5; Jer. 3:14, 31:31-33.

2. Jer. 3:8; Isa. 50:1; Hos. 2:2-13. In conjunction with Jeremiah, in Hosea we see

jealousy is actually quite graphic in several instances.[1]

It is even worthy of note that the divorce, relative to the plan of redemption in general, facilitates an important aspect of the process, though the subtle nuance of how it fits into the broader picture is not overly obvious. Whether deliberate or by happenstance, the severing of the marital relationship with Israel provided God the opportunity to withdraw himself from an isolated nationality of people. It was his stated intent from the giving of the promise to bless all the nations of the earth.[2]

And yet, God's known intentions notwithstanding, Abraham nevertheless became patriarch to the Jews, and the progenitor of a peculiar people to God.[3] The Gentiles were excluded from that.[4] They were treated as second class citizens in every respect. They were considered blemished and corrupted.[5] The Israelites were permitted to take slaves only from the heathen.[6] Food that wasn't fit for an Israelite was

---

that God acts every bit the part of an embittered ex-husband. "Go plead with your mother," he tells Hosea, "she is not my wife." He then rants about taking away everything she has; her corn and her wine, her oil, her silver and gold, that all came from him, but that she had attributed to Baalim. By leaving her desolate and destitute, exposing her lewdness, and taking away her mirth and her feasts, she would discover that it was better with God, her first husband, than with the many idols she pursued. So there is a very clear demonstration of God's separation from Israel, as well as a former espousement she shared with God, her first husband, that she now shared with another.

1. Jer. 2:20-24; Ezek. 16:15-38; et al.
2. Gen. 12:3, 22:15-18.
3. Gen. 12:3, 22:15-18; Gal. 3:7-9; Exod. 19:5-6; Deut. 14:2, 26:18-19.
4. Eph. 2:11-12.
5. Exod. 12:43, 48-49, 29:33; Lev. 22:10-12, 22:25.
6. Lev. 25:44.

served to the stranger in their gates, even though the law states that there was to be one law in the land, for the Israelite and stranger alike.[1] Only a Jew could be a king over the Jews.[2] Only a stranger could be charged usury.[3]

The nation of Israel was chosen by God and set above all the nations he made upon the earth, and the Gentiles were unable to be a part of them.[4] Israel had to be redefined if the Gentiles were to find a place amongst God's people.

And so this temporary break in the marriage made it possible to reestablish the covenant with broader national boundaries. From the moment the divorce itself was mentioned, God almost immediately spoke of not being angry forever.[5] He expressed a very blatant intent to entice Israel back to himself, and to betroth her again in mercy, with the door left wide open to a vast expansion in the understanding of Israel's true person.

Again, whether this was his deliberate intention or just a coincidence, there's no denying the end result. And I have a hard time accepting anything as a coincidence where God is concerned. He promised that all the nations would be blessed in Abraham.[6] He promised Christ the heathen for an inheritance.[7] Although it started with Abraham and the Jewish lineage, it has always been God's plan to save those who

---

1. Deut. 14:21; Exod. 12:49; Num. 15:16.
2. Deut. 17:14-15.
3. Deut. 23:20.
4. Exod. 19:5-6; Deut. 14:2, 26:18-19.
5. Jer. 3:1, 3:12-14.
6. Gen. 12:3, 22:15-18.
7. Ps. 2:7-8.

believe, and to make all the nations of the earth his people.[1]

> Therefore, behold, I will allure her, and bring her into the wilderness, and speak comfortably unto her. [...] And I will betroth thee unto me for ever; yea, I will betroth thee unto me in righteousness, and in judgment, and in lovingkindness, and in mercies. I will even betroth thee unto me in faithfulness: and thou shalt know the LORD. [...] and I will have mercy upon her that had not obtained mercy; and I will say to them which were not my people, Thou art my people; and they shall say, Thou art my God.[2]

Those who were not his people, he would call his people. This ties directly into the notion of the other nations being grafted into Israel. It is with Israel that the covenant is made. It is Israel he entices. It is Israel he betroths. And those who were not formerly his people, he would call his people, thereby bringing the other nations into the marriage bond and including them as part of the true Israel. Paul, in fact, quotes this same passage in Hosea, arguing for Gentile inclusion.[3]

He also explains that the good tree that is Israel has natural branches that were broken off in unbelief, wild branches that have been grafted in *through* belief, and natural branches formerly broken off that might be grafted back in *if* they believe.[4] In Christ there is neither Jew nor Gentile.[5]

---

1. Jn. 3:16.
2. Hos. 2:14-23.
3. Rom. 9:23-26; cf. Hos. 2:23, 1:10.
4. Rom. 11:17-24, esp. vv. 20 & 23.
5. Gal. 3:28.

The Relationship

Religious, ethnic, and genealogical affiliations prior to Christ are tossed to the wind. As Jesus said, God can raise up children to Abraham from the stones of the earth.[1] And from Paul, if you are Christ's, then you are Abraham's seed.[2] The true Jew is the one who is a Jew inwardly.[3] Thus, all those who believe by faith are of the same standing. It is solely by faith that even the Jews themselves become or remain a part of the nation of Israel, and Paul is very conspicuous in saying so.

> For they *are* not all Israel, which are of Israel: Neither, because they are the seed of Abraham, *are they* all children: but, In Isaac shall thy seed be called. That is, They which are the children of the flesh, these *are* not the children of God: but the children of the promise are counted for the seed.[4]

And so, again, the divorce severed the limited ties of the marriage bond between God and the physical nation of Israel, allowing a broader definition of Israel's identity based on faith. The nation that spurned him, he would have mercy upon, even as God says that a remnant would be saved, while the nations that knew him not, he would embrace.[5] Although we all recognize that there is an actual, physical nation of Israel that exists to this day, the true Israel, by a scriptural definition, is spiritual, and encompasses all nationalities. It

---

1. Matt. 3:9.
2. Gal. 3:29.
3. Rom. 2:28-29.
4. Rom. 9:6-8.
5. Isa. 10:20-23; Jer. 23:3-8; Hos. 2:14-23; Ps. 2:8.

is not the Jew by birth who is a child of God, but the Jew by faith who becomes the child of promise and the true seed of Abraham.[1] Israel is the spiritual nation of believers through faith. We are all God's wife through the new betrothal, as many of us as believe.

But getting back to the original point ... Israel, the spiritual nation of believers, is married to God, and this is extremely important to the dynamics of salvation. It not only plays a significant role on the grander scale, but also facilitates a oneness with God, which has its own distinct benefits. As Paul says, "we are members of his body, of his flesh, and of his bones. For this cause shall a man leave his father and mother, and shall be joined unto his wife, and they two shall be one flesh. This is a great mystery: but I speak concerning Christ and the church."[2] The marriage between Christ and the church is a great mystery, and it is repeatedly mentioned throughout the New Testament. Paul, for example, says to the Corinthians that he is jealous over them with godly jealousy, for he espoused them to one husband, that he may present them as a chaste virgin to Christ.[3] John the Baptist says that the bride belongs to the bridegroom, just as Jesus also makes use of the very same concept of the bride and bridegroom several times.[4] While the possible use of analogies or metaphors in these instances is not lost on me, a thorough comparison to other passages in the Old and New Testaments demonstrates a scriptural basis for their deliberate use.

---

1. Rom. 9:8.
2. Eph. 5:22-32.
3. 2 Cor. 11:2.
4. Jn. 3:29; Matt. 9:15, 25:1-13; Mk. 2:19-20; Lk. 5:34-35.

The Relationship

We have been given to Christ in marriage, reestablishing the severed bond God once shared with his people. Israel has been allured and comforted, betrothed in righteousness, judgment, and in lovingkindness. Mercy has been given to her who had not received mercy. And those who were not his people have become his people, and he their God. It is one of the pinnacle moments the world has waited for with 'bated breath.

> Let us be glad and rejoice, and give honour to him: for the marriage of the Lamb is come, and his wife hath made herself ready. And to her was granted that she should be arrayed in fine linen, clean and white: for the fine linen is the righteousness of saints.[1]

We are the body of Christ, the New Jerusalem, built upon the foundations of the apostles and prophets. We are built together as a habitation of God through the Spirit, fitly framed together and grown into a holy temple in the Lord. We are a bride adorned for our husband.[2]

Understanding our marriage bond is the beginning of understanding the New Testament.[3] It is more integral than most might imagine.

The marriage relationship, for example, goes a long way towards understanding the security we have in terms of salvation. Many young Christians, myself included once upon a time, question whether or not salvation can be lost. And

---

1. Rev. 19:7-8.
2. Rev. 21:2-3, 9-10; Eph. 2:11-13, 19-22.
3. Eph. 5:22-32.

truth be told, it's not an irrational fear. In fact, it's a healthy one, and spiritually-minded, since the fear of the Lord is the beginning of knowledge and wisdom. It is our duty to work out our own salvation with fear and trembling.[1]

But let me say very simply that you're not in any immediate spiritual danger if you're an active believer. The security of our salvation is the security of a marriage. No husband casts out his wife over simple mistakes. He might punish or scold her, just as Hebrews notes concerning believers, saying, "For whom the Lord loveth he chasteneth."[2] But nothing "shall be able to separate us from the love of God, which is in Christ Jesus our Lord."[3] If we sin, but still seek the Lord and strive to live a godly life, God forgives our mistakes for Christ's sake, who was the propitiation for our sins.[4]

Apart from apostasy, or crossing certain lines of extreme disobedience, like murdering someone, your salvation isn't going anywhere.[5] Our marriage is instrumental in the functionality of salvation, and God planned this covenant with care and precision at the dawn of creation. Christ himself tells us that fornication is the only acceptable reason to put away your wife.[6] God hates divorce, and has no desire to

---

1. Prov. 1:7, 9:10; Phil. 2:12.
2. Heb. 12:6; Prov. 3:12.
3. Rom. 8:38-39.
4. 1 Jn. 2:1-2.
5. Mk. 11:26; Matt. 18:21-35; Jms. 2:14-26; 1 Jn. 5:16-17; 2 Pet. 2:20-22; Heb. 6:4-6, 9-12; Matt. 13:3-9, 18-23. To abandon God and live a worldly life after receiving the truth is apostasy.
6. Matt. 5:31-32, 19:3-9; Mark 10:2-12; Jer. 2:20-24; Ezek. 16:15-38; Jer. 3:8. God put up with Israel's idolatry for a *very* long time before finally giving her a bill of divorce.

be rid of us.[1] He is not waiting for us to sin so he can cast us out. He's begging us not to walk away, or to live a life he can't be part of. He doesn't expect us to never make a mistake. Quite the contrary. He knows that we very well might. That's part of the reason Christ was sent to die.

Even those who rage against the concept of eternal security, or "once saved, always saved" as some term it, who complain about it being a "license to sin," etc., find themselves asking for, and expecting, forgiveness when they err, which they inevitably do. The fact is, as God well knows, becoming a mature and refined Christian is a process, and it takes time.[2] It doesn't happen overnight. Some travel the path more quickly. Others, not so much so. But if we are seeking the Lord, the path of our spiritual evolution is inevitable, and our salvation secure in the bond of marriage.

The marriage is also vital in navigating the unnecessary confusion surrounding concepts like righteousness, justification, and sanctification. The lengths to which some people have gone to explain them borders on insanity.

Because of the marriage, Christ is the rule of measure regarding these things.[3] In marriage, a man and woman become one flesh. This is more than an act of carnality, especially in the union between Christ and his bride. He who is

---

[1] Mal. 2:14-16.

[2] 2 Pet. 1:5-7. This passage gives an excellent example of the process of spiritual maturity. Add to our faith, virtue, knowledge, temperance, patience, godliness, brotherly kindness, and love. As a mature Christian, it is my observation that this is an inevitable process of spiritual evolution that develops over time.

[3] 1 Cor. 6:11, 7:14; 1 Tim. 3:16.

joined unto the Lord is one flesh and one spirit.[1] We have been gathered together in Christ as one body.[2] What he is, so too are we. While I wouldn't go so far as to say that *we* are Jesus Christ — he obviously retains his own individual identity — we are nevertheless treated as though we were. We are one person in the eyes of God.

This is why "no man cometh unto the Father" but by Jesus Christ.[3] Only he is truly pure and sanctified, justified, and righteous enough to stand before God. If you aren't part of Christ, and viewed in the eyes of God as Christ himself, you cannot stand before the throne of God. Lacking the oneness gained by our marriage to Christ, we stand on our own, naked and unworthy. By our own justification, we will be found wanting, for no flesh is justified in God's sight.[4] By our own attempts at sanctification, to cleanse and purify our daily lives, our own righteousness is yet as filthy rags.[5] We can't undo the past, or cleanse, on our own, the stain of the sins we have committed. Only God can do that.[6]

But by the oneness of our marriage bond, through faith we are, again, one flesh and one spirit. His purity, perfection, and righteousness are our own. We are one body, regarded and judged as one person. We are told to walk in sanctification, though we are sanctified already, because Christ is

---

1. 1 Cor. 6:15-17.
2. Eph. 1:10.
3. Jn. 14:6.
4. Acts 13:39; Rom. 3:19-20; Gal. 2:16.
5. Isa. 64:6.
6. Eph. 5:26; 1 Jn. 1:7, 9.

sanctified, and we are seen as Christ.[1] We seek to be justified by our actions and our obedience, though we are justified already, because Christ is justified, and we are seen as Christ.[2] We are told to be righteous, and yet, we are righteous already, because Christ is righteous, and we are seen as Christ. As one body, we are all sanctified and justified, by him and through him.[3] The righteousness of Christ is our own. Thus, when we stand before the throne of God, it is, in principle, Christ that will be judged, not us, being himself the head of the body, of which we are all part, rendering us of equal standing with his own quality and perfection. He is our advocate and our propitiation.[4] He is us. We are him. We are one.

---

1. 1 Cor. 1:2, 6:11; Heb. 2:11, 10:10, 10:14; 1 Thes. 4:4; Jude 1:1.
2. Acts 13:39; Rom. 3:21-28; Gal. 2:16.
3. 1 Cor. 7:14; Heb. 2:11, 10:10, 10:14.
4. 1 Jn. 2:1-2.

5

The Annulling

With the backdrop fully in place, let's now discuss the necessity of the sacrifice, and why the death of the one man was able to stand as a worthy ransom for all those who believe. That *is* the million-dollar question. How can Christ, through his singular death, legally bear the sins of the entire world, past, present and future?

To understand how it works, you have to begin by opening your mind to a new way of thinking. Most of us are taught that Christ was a heavenly version of the Old Testament sin offering. He was a spotless lamb who came and died for our sins.[1] The far-reaching application and effect of *his* sacrifice versus that of animals was merely a byproduct of his status as the son of God. Heavenly things require better sacrifices, so his greater sacrifice had a greater result.[2]

However, while there is some truth to this line of reasoning, it assigns too much focus and priority on the parallels

---

1. Jn. 1:29.
2. Heb. 9:23.

to legalistic rituals, and neglects the stated purpose of his death. Christ fulfilled any number of such parallels. He is the word made flesh, the very image of the heavenly patterns foreshadowed in the law.[1] As such, these parallels are to be expected.

We know, for example, that he was our Passover. The time of his death is consistent with the Passover.[2] He arrived in Jerusalem on lamb selection day.[3] When the soldiers came to break the bones of the crucified prisoners, he was already dead, so his bones were not broken, which follows the statutes of the Passover.[4] Paul even says that "Christ our passover is sacrificed for us."[5]

Christ likewise died as a worthy offering, sacrificing himself so he could enter the very presence of God, the heavenly holy of holies, and make atonement for the world as the high priest would do on the Day of Atonement.[6] He is our high priest, according to the order of Melchisedec, who was

---

1. Jn. 1:1, 14; Heb. 10:1.

2. Matt. 26:17-21; Mk. 14:12-18; Lk. 22:7-15. I do not mean to say that Christ died on the 14th day of the month according to the actual Passover ritual, but that he died during the general time of year in which the Passover festival occurred. The scriptures are clear that Jesus kept the Passover with his disciples. His crucifixion, therefore, took place on the following day, on the 15th.

3. Jn. 12:1, 12; Jn. 19:32-36; Exod. 12:46; Num. 9:12; Ps. 34:20. Jesus arrived in Bethany six days before the Passover. The Passover was on the 14th day of the month (Exod. 12:6). Six days before that, counting inclusively in the manner of a first century Jew, he would have arrived in Bethany on the 9th day of the month. He then entered Jerusalem the next day, on the 10th day of the month, which was the day the lambs were chosen (Exod. 12:3).

4. Jn. 19:31-37; Num. 9:12; Ps. 34:20.

5. 1 Cor. 5:7.

6. Lev. 16:2-6, 11, 15; Heb. 9:6-7, 11-12.

"without father, without mother, without descent, having neither beginning of days, nor end of life; but made like unto the Son of God."[1] And in the interest of pointing out the futility of trying to impose parallelisms on the significance of Christ's sacrifice, it is worth noting in this instance that the high priest first made a sacrifice for himself on the Day of Atonement. It purified him before entering into the presence of God, where he would *then* make intercession on behalf of the people.[2] Christ offered his own self as a perfect sacrifice to gain access to the throne of God.[3] His intercession on our behalf, according to the Day of Atonement ritual, was a related, but separate act. In other words, his death in this specific parallel was not a sacrifice intended for us, but for himself.

Our atonement was fulfilled through yet another parallel. In addition to being the high priest, Christ was also the scapegoat associated with the Day of Atonement. The high priest would select two goats. Lots would be cast, and the scapegoat would have the sins of the people laid upon its head and be led out of town.[4] Christ, the son of God the Father, and Barabbas, "son of the father," stood before the people, paralleling the two goats.[5] Jesus, chosen to be the scapegoat, was led out of town with the sins of the people, wearing

---

1. Heb. 7:1-17.
2. Lev. 16:2-6, 11, 15.
3. Heb. 9:6-7, 11-12.
4. Lev. 16:5, 7-10, 21-22.
5. Bar (βαρ) is a prefix meaning "son of." For interpretive comparison, see Jn. 1:42, 21:15-17 with Matt. 16:17. Peter is Simon, son of Jona, or Simon Barjona. Acts 4:36 also mentions Joses, who was surnamed Barnabas, which interprets as the son of consolation. Abba (αββα) means father. Thus, βαρ-

a crimson cord of blood around his head from the crown of thorns, in an extended fulfillment of the priestly laws and practices.[1]

There are many parallels I could list, though others require more extensive discourse. Suffice it to say, Christ's fulfillment of these things was inevitable. The sacrifices and rituals were designed according to the pattern of what was to come. Until Christ came and the heavenly application of the traditions was put into action, the mystery of their purpose remained veiled and hidden.[2]

Thus, the parallels have no real bearing on the purpose of his sacrifice. In fact, the opposite is closer to the truth. While the comparisons to the Old Covenant law may be valid in their own right, and while his sacrifice may have accomplished the intended legal purpose for each, none of these analogous parallels are the stated reason for his death, which is composed of two individual parts; viz. the legal reason for his death, and what resulted from his death.

Beginning first with the latter, Christ, by his own mouth, specified that his blood was shed to establish the New Covenant, which Hebrews readily confirms.[3] A testament — as in a "last will and testament" — is not in force until the death of the testator. So long as Christ lived, there could not be a New Testament. It would have remained unrealized.

αββα, is the son of the father, βαρ-αββας (Bar-Abbas).

1. Talmud, *Yoma* 41b. It is taught in rabbinical tradition that, "he (the high priest) tied a tongue of crimson wool to the head of the goat that was to be sent away [the scapegoat]."

2. Matt. 13:35; Rom. 16:25; Eph. 3:9; Col. 1:26; 1 Cor. 2:7-8.

3. Heb. 9:15-17.

And he took the cup, and gave thanks, and gave *it* to them, saying, Drink ye all of it; For this is my blood of the new testament, which is shed for many for the remission of sins.[1]

And he took the cup, and when he had given thanks, he gave *it* to them: and they all drank of it. And he said unto them, This is my blood of the new testament, which is shed for many.[2]

Likewise also the cup after supper, saying, This cup *is* the new testament in my blood, which is shed for you.[3]

After the same manner also *he took* the cup, when he had supped, saying, This cup is the new testament in my blood: this do ye, as oft as ye drink *it*, in remembrance of me.[4]

The other half of his death is the yang to the yin. You can't make a new covenant without first disposing of the old one. A "new" covenant, as Hebrews says, makes the first "old," so that it is ready to vanish away.[5] Like any other contract, there is a necessity to void the previous agreement. Thus, the scriptures tell us in plain language that, "He taketh away the first, that he may establish the second."[6] In so doing, there was "a disannulling of the commandment going before for the weakness and unprofitableness thereof,"

---

1. Matt. 26:27-28.
2. Mk. 14:23-24.
3. Lk. 22:20.
4. 1 Cor. 11:25.
5. Heb. 10:9-10, 7:12.
6. Heb. 8:13.

The Annulling

which he then replaced with something new, "built upon a better hope and upon better promises."[1] Christ voided the Old Covenant, replacing it with something new, so that our obligation is no longer to the former, but to the latter.[2] Otherwise, there would be legal ambiguities, not unlike the ones we often encounter in our doctrines, due to the fact that people fail to recognize the transition.

This notable theme of the law's dissolution throughout Paul's letters, most especially in Romans and Galatians, is the foundation of one of the more heated debates in modern Christendom. Since we are no longer "under the law" but "under grace," do we still need to keep the law of Moses? And the simplest answer is no, at least from the perspective that the law of Moses is no longer the active covenant.[3] With the establishment of the New Covenant and the disannulling of the Old, the law has been superseded. It no longer exercises authority over us.[4] Christ mediated a New Covenant, and to reiterate, he "taketh away the first, that he may establish the second."[5]

The Old Covenant is gone for those in Christ.

And in taking away the Old to establish the New, he necessarily voided the oath that went with it, which is the subtle and elusive key to the whole act of redemption. As it says in Hebrews, it was by means of his death, which was done for the redemption of the transgressions under the Old

---

1. Heb. 7:18-19, 8:6.
2. Heb. 10:9-10; Col. 2:13-14; Eph. 2:14-16.
3. Acts 15:5-29.
4. Rom. 7:1-6; .
5. Heb. 9:15, 10:9-10.

Testament, that we are now able to receive the promise of eternal inheritance offered by the New Testament, which couldn't be in force while he lived.[1] Voiding our oath initiated the provisionary loophole mentioned in chapter two. It obligated him by law to bear our sins as a consequence, which he couldn't otherwise have done. This sort of surrogate responsibility is not possible within the basic purview of the law. As I previously said, you have to dismiss the parallels to animal sacrifices and such. No man can serve as a ransom for another.

> None *of them* can by any means redeem his brother, nor give to God a ransom for him: (For the redemption of their soul *is* precious, and it ceaseth for ever:) That he should still live for ever, *and* not see corruption.[2]

However, a *husband* can serve as a ransom for his *wife*, specifically in the case of a vow or an oath. This is why the previous discussion of our relationship with God was important. The marriage bond is the only way to accomplish what was accomplished.

> If a man vow a vow unto the LORD, or swear an oath to bind his soul with a bond; he shall not break his word, he shall do according to all that proceedeth out of his mouth. […] If a woman also vow a vow unto the LORD, and bind herself by a bond […] And if she had at all an husband, when she vowed, or uttered ought out of her lips, wherewith she bound her soul; And her husband heard *it,* and held his peace at her

---

1. Heb. 9:15-17.
2. Ps. 49:7-9.

in the day that he heard *it*: then her vows shall stand, and her bonds wherewith she bound her soul shall stand. But if her husband disallowed her on the day that he heard *it*; then he shall make her vow which she vowed, and that which she uttered with her lips, wherewith she bound her soul, of none effect: and the LORD shall forgive her. [...] Every vow, and every binding oath to afflict the soul, her husband may establish it, or her husband may make it void. But if her husband altogether hold his peace at her from day to day; then he establisheth all her vows, or all her bonds, which *are* upon her: he confirmeth them, because he held his peace at her in the day that he heard *them*. But if he shall any ways make them void after that he hath heard *them*; then he shall bear her iniquity.[1]

As our husband, God had the authority to void our oath when we first made it, rendering us guiltless. But rather than void it, he boldly confirmed and established our oath with an oath of his own, swearing to render judgement. In which case, relative to what Christ did, disannulling the Old Covenant and the associated oath, not only *could* Christ serve as a ransom, the law demanded it. Having held his peace, and then making the law and the oath void after the fact, he was required to bear our iniquity.

That is why Christ had to die. *That* is why he was made to bear our iniquity. We were dead in our sins as oath-breakers. We were transgressors under the covenant. With God sworn to judgement and unable to take his own name in vain, the only way to save us from that judgement was to void the covenant and oath that made us guilty as sinners and oath-

---

1. Num. 30:2-3, 6-8, 13-15.

breakers, and then bear the resulting burden of our iniquity himself. So Christ "[blotted] out the handwriting of ordinances that was against us, which was contrary to us, and took it out of the way...."[1] He abolished the law of commandments in his own flesh, nailing it to the cross, so that all those who believe would be reconciled to God.[2]

So understand that although many things were fulfilled in the process of establishing the New Covenant, the parallels to base sacrifices of atonement and forgiveness are incidental. He didn't die because he was a Passover sacrifice. He didn't die because he was a scapegoat. He didn't die as some random sin offering. God, declaring the end from the beginning, gave us the ritual of the scapegoat to show how Christ would one day be displayed with a criminal and be led out of town with the sins of the people. God gave us the example of the Passover to show how death would one day pass over those who are covered with the blood of Christ. God required the high priest to make a sacrifice to enter the holy of holies to show how Christ would one day sacrifice himself for that same honor.

They are all examples of heavenly things, and not the very image of the things themselves.[3] *Christ* is the heavenly thing, and the law is paralleling his accomplishments, not the other way around. What he would one day do, the law reflects. It is the pattern and process by which he would do it that the law seeks to mimic.

Once you understand this simple truth, that Christ didn't

---

1. Col. 2:14.
2. Eph. 2:15-16; Col. 2:14.
3. Heb. 8:5, 10:1.

die to fulfill specific rituals of the law, but to replace one covenant with another, you can begin to see the light at the end of the tunnel. The purpose of his death, and the shedding of his blood, was to bring about a covenantal shift.[1] This is the Holy Grail of understanding. That's what made the sacrifice necessary. That's what makes salvation work. It's all about the shift. He died because he voided the Old Covenant, bearing our iniquity in the process. And once he was dead, his testament was empowered, establishing the New Covenant, so that all who believe could receive eternal life.

That is what he died to accomplish. And this reality is an important distinction. If he died to be our scapegoat, or some other sin offering, our sins would indeed have been forgiven, until we sinned again. But his sacrifice "put away sin" once and for all and condemned it — all sin, past, present, and future — because his death paid the price demanded by the law to disannul the covenant that defined our sins and condemned us.[2]

So there was an actual necessity for God's own death in accordance with the law, due to the sins that he had to bear. That's why he came to us as Jesus Christ, the man. God can't die, so the Word of God, his very utterance, took upon himself the form of a humble servant, making himself a little lower than the angels, and became a man, "for the suffering of death," that, "he by the grace of God should taste death for every man."[3]

The "Lamb of God," or more simply, "God's Lamb,"

---

1. Heb. 9:15-23.
2. Heb. 9:26-28; Rom. 8:3.
3. Heb. 2:9, 16; Phil. 2:6-11; cf. Isa. 45:21-23.

wasn't a spiritual lamb sent by God for *us*. God sent the lamb for himself, presented as his own spotless sin offering. While God himself had no sin of his own, he still took upon himself the burden and responsibility of our iniquity all the same, which comes with the price of death and curses.[1] So he sent his own "lamb" to die in his place, laying upon that lamb the iniquity of the world. The oath-breaker must die, so Christ died. And he died on the cross in particular, because the oath-breaker must be cursed, and it is written, "Cursed is every one that hangeth on a tree," whereby he became a curse for us.[2]

Thus, Jesus was, indeed, the Lamb of God, and he did, indeed, take away the sins of the world. But he didn't do that by dying as a sin offering for us. He did it by dying as a sin offering for God, who bore the sins of the world.

The end result is that God declared, and his law demanded, that we must die for sin, and so we died, because we are one with Christ. His law demanded that we must be cursed, and so we were cursed, because we are one with Christ. His death was our death, and his curse was our curse, so that every jot and tittle has been fulfilled for everyone who believes. When Christ said that "Till heaven and earth pass, one jot or one tittle shall in no wise pass from the law, till all be fulfilled," he did not mean that he, or anyone else, had to emulate every act and commandment of the law.[3] Rather, for every living soul, "fulfilling all" is about following the natural and legal course of the law to the bitter end. The law

---

1. Deut. 27:26, 30:19.

2. Jn. 1:1, 14; Gal. 3:13; Deut. 21:22-23.

3. Matt. 5:18.

promises life or death, blessing or cursing.[1] Those under the law who are found to be transgressors are condemned, and the natural and legal end consequence for such under the law is death and curses. So we are buried with Christ in baptism, and made dead *through* him so that we might be resurrected in the newness of life.[2] The old man is crucified with Christ, and hanged on a tree, cursed by the law. We are then "born again" as new creations, born first in the flesh by our mother, and again in the spirit, being quickened together with Christ.[3] So by Christ's death and by Christ's curse, both he and we have fulfilled the law according to its ultimate purpose, bringing it to its concluding finality by the crucifixion of Christ. Our sins have been paid for in full. The declaration in the garden has been satisfied.

In the eyes of the law, we are dead.[4]

And that's really the genius of it all. Flesh and blood cannot inherit the kingdom of God.[5] Salvation is not about escaping death. It is about embracing it, so we can be reborn in the newness of life. We weren't merely forgiven by the sacrifice of a spiritual lamb. Such a view is an oversimplification. We were altogether set free from the condemnation of the law via its completion and disannulment.

The process of salvation takes us from one creation to the next. There are two lives, natural and spiritual; two

---

1. Deut. 30:19.
2. Rom. 6:4-7; Col. 2:12-13.
3. Jn. 3:3-8; Eph. 2:5; Col. 2:13.
4. Rom. 6:3-11, 7:4; Gal. 2:19-20.
5. 1 Cor. 15:50.

births, flesh and spirit; two creations, terrestrial and heavenly; and two Adams from which we descend.[1] In Christ, we are descended from the new Adam, free from the promise of death in the garden, to live in a spiritual world where the law has no dominion, and where God's declaration has been satisfied.

This is the root of the law versus grace concept. By his declaration, God was obligated to deliver us to death. By his law, he was obligated to render judgement. The old man of the flesh must die.[2] This is the law. It is the ministry of death and condemnation. There has to be an amends for our transgressions.

But having been slain through the propitiation of Christ's own death, God's word and law have been fulfilled. As new creations descended from a new Adam, living in a new spiritual world, God's hand is no longer forced to judgement. God can *now* simply say, "I forgive you," and let that be the end of it. This is the condition of being under grace. It is the undeserved, freely given mercy and favor of God in our lives, through good times and bad, through our successes *and* our failings, whereas being formerly bound by his own word and oath, such mercy was not previously possible under his declaration or under his law.

We had to die before we could live.

And so by faith we die, and by faith we live, though it

---

1. 1 Cor. 15:44; Jn. 3:5-6; Rev. 21:1; 1 Cor. 15:45-47. As discussed in chapter four, the New Jerusalem (Rev. 21:2; Eph. 2:11-13, 19-22), which is on the new earth (21:1-2), is the bride of Christ (21:9-10), which is us.

2. Rom. 6:6; Col. 3:9.

is not we who live, but Christ who lives in us.[1] We have been born again as new creations, living under grace rather than law, where the price of our iniquity has already been borne and satisfied, and where God is no longer obligated, by declaration or law, to impute our transgressions to us.[2]

> Surely he hath borne our griefs, and carried our sorrows: yet we did esteem him stricken, smitten of God, and afflicted. But he *was* wounded for our transgressions, *he was* bruised for our iniquities: the chastisement of our peace *was* upon him; and with his stripes we are healed. All we like sheep have gone astray; we have turned every one to his own way; and the LORD hath laid on him the iniquity of us all. [...] By his knowledge shall my righteous servant justify many; for he shall bear their iniquities.[3]

---

1. Gal. 2:20.
2. Rom. 4:3-8.
3. Isa. 53:4-12.

6

The Ä´gə-pā´ Principle

What comes next is by far the hardest part for most to grasp. Our sins have been taken away and forgiven. Intercession for our future sins has fallen beneath the umbrella of God's grace and mercy. The law is voided and gone, written now on our hearts and minds. Our lives are now conscience-driven, as in the days before the full establishment of the law, where every man did what was right in his own eyes.[1] So what, exactly, are God's expectations for us in this New Covenant? What rules are we supposed to follow? What is the proper way to live, act, behave, and so on?

I like to consider our current state a case of complicated simplicity. The problem we now deal with is the undeniable fact that the law of Moses is gone, and that we need not keep it or adhere to it, while at the same time being faced with the dilemmic and preposterous question of which part of "you shall not kill" we intend not to keep.

When dealing with the issue of not being "under the

---

1. Heb. 8:10; Jer. 31:33; Rom. 2:15; Deut. 12:8.

law," but "under grace," questions of this nature come up time and again. The Ten Commandments, and other laws that still have some viable application in the present day, are founded in common sense principles. I can't think of a Christian out there who would disagree with the fact that we should not murder or commit adultery, worship other gods, covet that which belongs to our neighbor, etc. Again, it's common sense.

And yet, according to Paul, if we do keep any part of the law, we are then debtors to do the whole law.[1] We can't decide to keep some laws, but not others. It's all or nothing. James tells us that to offend in any one point makes us guilty of the whole thing. If we don't commit adultery, but we do kill, we are transgressors of the law all the same, because the same law that said "do not commit adultery" also said "do not kill."[2] So when we keep the commandment, "you shall not kill," it has the inescapable consequence of making us every bit as culpable as a murderer the moment we fail in anything else, no matter how trivial. The fact is, the commandments give life to sin, and this is without exception.

Paul even goes so far as to demonstrate that the Ten Commandments themselves, however holy, just, and good as they may be, result in our spiritual death. It's not just the seemingly pointless rituals, like ceremonial cleansing, circumcision, etc. Nor is Paul referring exclusively to the Rabbinical commandments, which, as Christ noted, were sometimes contrary to the laws of God. Paul said he didn't know lust until he received the commandment, "you shall not

---

1. Gal. 5:3.
2. Jms. 2:10-11.

covet." And upon receiving this commandment, he went from being alive without it, to being dead by the sin that was quickened *through* it.[1] All the commandments of the law kill. To sin is to despise the covenant and the oath, and to keep the law is to give life to both. "The sting of death *is* sin; and the strength of sin *is* the law."[2]

As discussed in chapter two, the law's power of condemnation is a huge part of why it was given to us in the first place. It defined our sins and made them sinful, and obligated God by his oath, and by legal covenant, to impute to us our wrong-doings. At the same time, this is why the law was subsequently taken away, to expiate our sins by the disannulling of the very commandments that gave them life.[3] That's what Jesus died to accomplish. If we carry on believing that we have to keep the law, then his death was quite literally pointless.[4]

So we are faced with the complication that we shouldn't kill, but we can't keep, "you shall not kill." We shouldn't commit adultery, but we can't keep, "you shall not commit adultery." We shouldn't steal, but we can't keep, "you shall not steal."

And so the confusion begins.

Often as not, this unspoken difficulty leads most people to a very natural double standard. They tend to create a system of categorization, where some laws "were transferred to

---

1. Rom. 7:7-12.
2. 1 Cor. 15:56.
3. Rom. 7:8-9, 8:3; Heb. 7:18-19, 8:7-8; Col. 2:14.
4. Gal. 2:21.

the New Covenant," while others that are too severe, outdated, politically incorrect by today's standards, etc., fall into a dismissive category of, "well, that's from the Old Testament, and we're not 'under the law' anymore." So we're subject to the law when it suits them, but not when they disagree with the commandment in question. They think we should keep, "you shall not murder," but they don't necessarily think that we need to destroy our houses over mold, stone our daughters for sexual immorality, or that we should go outside the city limits to do our bathroom business in a hole.[1]

This compromise is, of course, entirely incongruous with the all-or-nothing principle of the law. Nevertheless, many Christians do find it to be a valid solution.[2] After all, there have to be *some* guidelines, right? So tattoos aren't allowed, because that seems kind of reasonable, but we're not going to cut off a woman's hand if she grabs a guy by his "secrets" in defense of her husband.[3] That's just too harsh. We'll stick to the restriction against pork, but it's not appropriate to make a rapist marry his victim.[4]

The fact is, as my wife once told me, "people want their rules and structure." Most of us inherently want someone to tell us what to do, what we can do, and what we cannot do. And so we end up with this fragmented concoction of the old law, smattered with our gospel of faith, and presented as part

---

1. Lev. 14:33-53; 23:12-14; Deut. 22:13-21.
2. Gal. 5:3; Jas. 2:10-11.
3. Lev. 19:28; Deut. 25:11-12
4. Lev. 11:7; Deut. 22:28-29.

of the selfsame New Covenant that made these very commandments null and void. As Paul says, we have rebuilt that which was destroyed. The end result is that the very rules and structure so many Christians crave, just as the Galatians did, comes with the unintended consequence of condemnation, and this point can't be emphasized or reiterated enough.[1] The letter of the law, even in the case of the Ten Commandments, results in spiritual death.[2]

So the task at hand is to learn to walk in "the law of the spirit of life" rather than "the law of sin and death."[3] That is what we have been called to preach and to live. The letter of the law kills. The ministry of the spirit is life and righteousness.[4] And it is our duty to do what we believe to be right and good.[5] That's what righteousness is. It is "right-doing," or more simply, "doing the right thing." It is living by faith rather than legalistically-derived obligation, by the which someone taught you that something is "commanded," so that a principle act or behavior intended for good becomes a law that is instead your undoing.[6] If you fail to do this "commandment," you are guilty of sin, made sinful by the commandment itself. And as an oath-breaker, entangled again by the law, God is compelled by his own word to judge you. The commandment becomes an instrument of condemnation

---

1. Gal. 3:1-5, 4:9-11, 4:21-31.
2. 2 Cor. 3:6-8; Rom. 7:7-12.
3. Rom. 8:1-2, 4.
4. 2 Cor. 3:6-9.
5. Jms. 4:17.
6. Gal. 2:21, 5:4. Rom. 7:10-11.

that prevents God from being merciful.[1]

We are either led and instructed by the Holy Spirit, or we are not.[2] We are either free from the law, or we are not.[3] Whether it be the law of Moses or a new law of our own making, which is invariably derived from the Old Testament, its very existence puts people under condemnation.[4] You can't have your cake and eat it too. It's either righteous living by faith, trusting in God's grace, or it's the law, along with the rigid consequences that come with it.

Just consider the issue that arose between Peter and Paul. Peter was teaching the Gentile disciples that they had to keep the law of Moses. But Paul "withstood him to the face," and admonished him in front of the entire group, saying that the law does nothing to make us righteous, but rather, makes us transgressors all over again, rendering Christ's death in vain.[5] Our modern church environment, in principle, is doing the exact same thing as Peter. We know that it's by faith, but we're being taught to keep certain laws, and Paul is here to say that if we think we'll find righteousness by capitulating to legalistic obligations, we frustrate the grace of God.

Never lose sight of the fact that the whole point of Christ's death was to disannul the Old Covenant and establish a New Covenant.[6] We have no obligation to the law of

---

1. Gal. 5:1-4.
2. 1 Jn. 2:27; Gal. 5:18.
3. Rom. 7:2-6, 8:2; Gal. 4:21-31.
4. Gal. 4:21-31.
5. Gal. 2:11-21.
6. Matt. 26:27-28; Mk. 14:23-24; Lk. 22:20; 1 Cor. 11:25; Heb. 7:12, 7:18-19,

Moses.¹ Apart from the lessons we can learn from it, it might as well not exist to us. The law is death. By voiding the law and the oath, and by taking our sins upon himself, Christ has made it possible for us to die and be born again, free from both the obligation and condemnation of the law, and free from God's declaration of death in the garden.²

While I realize that this is a difficult adjustment for many to make to their long-held beliefs, please understand that the scriptures are in no way unclear with regard to this subject. This *is* how it is. There is absolutely no ambiguity concerning our obligation to the law, or what the consequences will be if we find ourselves back under its bondage.

I've often heard the adage that "the greatest trick the Devil ever pulled was convincing the world he didn't exist."³ I would disagree. I believe that the greatest trick the Devil ever pulled was to convince those who were freed from the law that they were still in bondage to it. It is only by the law that the Devil has any power over us.⁴ Where there is no law, there is no transgression.⁵ The Devil's role in heaven was as

---

8:6, 10:9-10.

1. Acts 15:23-24.

2. Num. 30:15; Isa. 53:6, 11; Gal. 2:20; Rom. 6:4; Col. 2:12-13; Eph. 2:5; 1 Pet. 3:18; Jn. 3:3-6; Rom. 8:1-2; Gal. 5:1-4.

3. *The Usual Suspects*, 1995. Original quote from Charles Pierre Baudelaire, *The Generous Gambler*, 1864. "My dear brethren, do not ever forget, when you hear the progress of lights praised, that the loveliest trick of the Devil is to persuade you that he does not exist!"

4. 1 Cor. 15:56.

5. Rom. 4:15. A common misconception of this passage is that without the law there is no sin. It is more correct to say that without a law, there is no legally imputable offense to try and convict (cf. Rom. 5:13; sin is not imputed where there is no law, though sin existed apart from the law).

The Ä′gə-pā′ Principle

a prosecutor.[1] And as the scriptures state, there was no longer a place for him in heaven, who accused the brethren day and night before God. We overcame him by the blood of the lamb.[2] A prosecutor without a law can't convict anyone. In fact, if there is no law, the prosecutor doesn't even have a case to bring to trial.

That's the long and short of our circumstance. God repealed the law, so that sin was no longer legally imputable and convictable.[3] We now live a new life where we, as Christians, have learned what is right, and respect the goodness of the principle of the law, but without the condemnation of its binding authority.[4] The prosecutor has no case. Any attempt to accuse or condemn us with laws that don't exist are thrown out of court. Sin can't be imputed where there is no law.[5] And yet, the prosecutor tries to convince people to live by laws, both old and new, in what has been a very successful and aggressive campaign to reclaim his position and authority to accuse and convict us, and ultimately condemn us.

So understand that the true state of our being is that we are not obligated to the law, though we are not without some form of spiritual law to God.[6] We are not required to keep the law, though as Christians we will nevertheless fulfill it.[7]

---

1. Zech. 3:1-2; Rev. 12:8-10.
2. Rev. 12:8-10.
3. Jn. 1:1, 10-11, 14; Col. 2:9; Heb. 2:9, 16; Phil. 2:6-11; Matt. 26:27-28; Mk. 14:23-24; Lk. 22:20; 1 Cor. 11:25; Heb. 7:12, 18-19, 8:6, 10:9-10.
4. Rom. 3:21, 8:1-14; 1 Jn. 2:27, 3:6-9.
5. Rom. 5:13.
6. Rom. 6:14; 1 Cor. 9:21.
7. Acts 15:23-29; Rom. 13:8-10; Gal. 3:12, 5:14; 1 Jn. 3:9.

Our duty is to live lawfully *without* laws. It's like we're the walking embodiment of an Outback Steakhouse slogan. No rules. Just right.

But people have a hard time handling this. We've been set free, but instinctively desire a self-imposed form of bondage. The Galatians, as already mentioned, are known for this very thing, and almost the entirety of Paul's epistle to them speaks out against the imposition of the law versus righteous living by faith.[1] People *want* their rules and structure, but we have to cast out the bondwoman and her child.[2] To keep the law, even in the case of the Ten Commandments, is to be in bondage to spiritual death.

And this brings us full circle back to the original problem. What part of, "you shall not kill," "you shall not commit adultery," or, "you shall not steal," do any of us intend to not keep? We would all agree that we should not do these things. And that's what creates the confusion. We know to keep such laws. But at the same time, subjecting ourselves to them puts us under the whole of the law and the condemnation that comes with it.

So how do we keep the law without keeping the law?

I once asked this very question in prayer. I was feeling discouraged by failure. And although I had many years of scriptural knowledge in my head, I simply couldn't grasp the answer, though it was there in plain sight all along. I don't know why I never saw it. Perhaps I was too proud.[3]

In the end, it comes down to a very simple thing. We

---

1. Gal. 4:9-11.
2. Gal. 4:21, 30-31.
3. Jas. 4:6; 1 Pet. 5:5.

The Ä´gə-pā´ Principle

keep the law without keeping the law by living according to the principle upon which the law is based.[1]

> Jesus said unto him, Thou shalt love the Lord thy God with all thy heart, and with all thy soul, and with all thy mind. This is the first and great commandment. And the second *is* like unto it, Thou shalt love thy neighbour as thyself. On these two commandments hang all the law and the prophets.[2]

Love. It is the key to everything.[3] It is the spirit, or principle, behind the law itself, and is the manner and method by which we can live up to it.[4] It *is* the law.[5]

It is also the "new commandment" we were given by Christ as he made the New Covenant with the disciples.

> A new commandment I give unto you, That ye love one another; as I have loved you, that ye also love one another. By this shall all *men* know that ye are my disciples, if ye have love one to another.[6]

The Old Covenant came with rules at the time of its establishment, which were annulled along with the covenant itself. And with the ushering in of a New Covenant, so too were we given a new covenantal law. Love.

---

1. 2 Cor. 3:6. The spirit ($\pi\nu\varepsilon\tilde{\upsilon}\mu\alpha$) of the law is the applicable principle behind it.
2. Matt. 22:37-40.
3. 1 Cor. 13:1-13.
4. Rom. 13:8-10; Gal. 5:14; Jas. 2:8; 1 Pet. 1:22-25; 2 Pet. 1:3-10; 1 Jn. 2:10; 2 Cor. 3:6. The spirit ($\pi\nu\varepsilon\tilde{\upsilon}\mu\alpha$) of the law is the applicable principle behind it.
5. Matt. 7:12.
6. Jn. 13:34-35; cf. 1 Jn. 2:7, 3:11; 2 Jn. 1:5-6.

As I said before, for Christians, the law may as well not exist. While it does serve a valid purpose in understanding righteous behavior, the New Covenant rule is the foundation for the entirety of the Old Covenant law.[1] Love is our commandment now.[2] It is the message we heard from the beginning.[3] It's the Golden Rule. If you can understand this, then you can understand the law, because the law's whole purpose was to teach and enforce this very thing.

From the moment this became clear, my entire perspective changed. Concepts in scripture that had always seemed so difficult suddenly made sense. Passages that seemed impossible, and that had formerly filled me with an indefinable conviction, I found myself agreeing with. I realized that love is the narrow path so few ever find.[4]

> Therefore all things whatsoever ye would that men should do to you, do ye even so to them: for this is the law and the prophets.[5]

> For all the law is fulfilled in one word, *even* in this; Thou shalt love thy neighbour as thyself.[6]

> Owe no man any thing, but to love one another: for he that loveth another hath fulfilled the law. For this, Thou shalt not

---

1. Matt. Matt. 7:12, 22:37-40.
2. Jn. 13:34-35; cf. 1 Jn. 2:7, 3:11; 2 Jn. 1:5-6.
3. Rom. 7:12; 2 Tim. 3:16; cf. Matt. 22:36-40; Rom. 13:8-10; 1 Jn. 2:7, 3:11; 2 Jn. 1:5-6.
4. Matt. 7:13-14.
5. Matt. 7:12.
6. Gal. 5:14.

commit adultery, Thou shalt not kill, Thou shalt not steal, Thou shalt not bear false witness, Thou shalt not covet; and if *there be* any other commandment, it is briefly comprehended in this saying, namely, Thou shalt love thy neighbour as thyself. Love worketh no ill to his neighbour: therefore love *is* the fulfilling of the law.[1]

This is a recurrent theme throughout the New Testament, and everything else falls into place when you apply it.[2] We don't need to be commanded, "do not kill." We are commanded to love our neighbor as ourselves. Since love works no ill, a Christian practicing love will not murder someone. Neither will they steal from them, sleep with their spouse, sue them for their possessions, give false testimony against them, etc. If we love God, we will not worship another. If we love our parents, we will take care of them when they are old, and thus honor them.

So what part of "you shall not kill" should we not keep? We shouldn't keep any part of it at all. Why? Because the commandment *no longer exists*. That's what people need to come to terms with. The moment the New Covenant was made, and the Old Covenant voided, the commandments contained in the Old Covenant ceased to be. You can't keep, "you shall not kill," because there *is* no such commandment. For Christians, there is only, "love your neighbor as yourself," and people who walk in love won't kill anyone. It's really that simple.

As I said from the beginning of this chapter, it's a case

---

1. Rom. 13:8-10.
2. Jas. 2:8; 1 Pet. 1:19-25; 1 Jn. 3:22-23, 5:2; 2 Jn. 1:5.

of complicated simplicity. It all seems so confusing, keeping the law without keeping the law, until you realize that there *is* no law, only the principle behind it, which is both its fulfillment and its replacement.

That being said, if we consider topics like going to church, tithing, etc., which are some of the most prolific "commandments" bandied about by Christians of all types, understand that we should do these things for the right reasons. We should do them according to the agape principle, which is selfless, magnanimous love.

We should go to church so we can support and inspire our brothers and sisters in the faith when they face trials and hardships, which is precisely the reason Hebrews encourages us not to forsake the assembling of ourselves together.[1] We should go to church because it gives us an opportunity to engage in praise and worship, and to hear the word spoken and taught by someone called by God to be the shepherd of a flock.[2] We should go to church because our assemblies create a core of support for our faith in general, whereas the lack of such assemblies would inevitably lead to our faith being scattered to the winds.

We should not be going to church because of any inferred "commandment" to do so, but for the love, encouragement, and benefit of our church community.[3]

Neither should we be tithing because of any commandment to give ten percent. The ten percent of a person's increase, in its Biblical context, is the Levite inheritance, and

---

[1]. Heb. 10:24-25.
[2]. Eph. 4:11; 1 Cor. 12:27-28.
[3]. Acts 20:7; Heb. 10:24-25.

nothing more. Eleven tribes got land. The Levites got a tenth of everyone else's "income," whether it was in the form of money, crops, livestock, etc.[1] Unless your preacher is a Levite serving in the Temple or Tabernacle of the Lord, and you are an Israelite under the Old Covenant, living and earning on your parcel of inherited land, the ten percent law doesn't apply to you, and it never has.

Paul tells us that we should give as we are able, as we have purposed in our hearts, and "… not by commandment."[2] We should give because the church staff works all week to provide a variety of services, and they have earned their income.[3] We should give because the minister of the church has earned a fair wage instructing the congregation and seeing to their spiritual edification.[4] We should give so the church has the means to help those in need.[5]

It is also worth saying that if you are a member of a church, it's not free to maintain the ministry or the facility. The electricity, water, telephone, internet, website, mortgage, insurance, etc., all cost money. The music equipment, video monitors, PA system and other necessities cost money. The incidentals, like coffee and donuts, office supplies, weekly flyers, programs or pamphlets … everything costs money. If you enjoy the services your church provides, which have been maintained through untold hours of dedicated work, and many dollars spent, then it is a good thing

---

1. Lev. 27:32; Num. 18:20-24, 26:52-62.
2. 2 Cor. 8:12-13, 9:7, 8:8.
3. 1 Cor. 9:9-10, 13; 1 Tim. 5:18; Lev. 19:13; Deut. 24:15, 25:4.
4. 1 Cor. 9:3-14, spec. 9:14.
5. 2 Cor. 9:10-13; Rom. 12:13.

to participate in the financial burden, whether it be ten percent of your earnings or ninety percent, as each of us is able.

In short, there are a thousand reasons why we should give to our church, each righteous, each commendable, and each borne out of love. A commandment to give ten percent of our income is not one of them.

And truth be told, if pastors presented the tithing necessity as they should, more people would likely give. The stigma of greed in the church is infamous. People don't want to tithe their grocery money so the pastor can drive a Mercedes, while they themselves struggle to make ends meet. If people knew what they were giving to, they might be more inclined to give.

But understand that all the commandments have a fundamental foundation in love.[1] Love is patient and kind. It is not envious, overbearing or proud. It does not behave unseemly or selfishly. It is not easily provoked, thinks no evil, and does not rejoice in iniquity, but in the truth. Love bears all things, believes all things, hopes all things, and endures all things. Love never fails.[2]

We have gone from the vast array of laws that only one man ever managed to keep, to two simple and interdependent commandments that constitute the true spirit of the law. All the law and the prophets depend upon them.[3] Vain deeds done by tradition, commandment, or obligation rather than

---

1. Matt. 7:12, 22:37-40; Gal. 5:14; Rom. 13:8-10.
2. 1 Cor. 13:4-8.
3. Matt. 22:37-40.

The Ä´gə-pā´ Principle | 83

love are pointless.[1] We should love God, and love our neighbor, with the former fulfilled by the latter. We demonstrate our love for God by keeping his commandments, which is done by loving our neighbor.[2] Ergo, we have but a single applicable commandment, to love our neighbor as ourselves, as Christ taught us. This is how people will know that we are his disciples.[3]

---

1. 1 Cor. 13:1-3.
2. 1 Jn. 5:2-3.
3. Jn. 13:34-35.

7

Ancillary Issues

I know that for some, this is a lot to digest, and I have found that there are often follow-up questions people ask, either due to confusion caused by lingering perceptions, or just for simple clarification. Additionally, while most people can usually grasp how it all works once they see it laid out, and are usually quite receptive to the simplicity of it all, there are nevertheless points of denominational bias or dogma that they have a hard time reconciling with some of what has been discussed.

I have also come across people who are simply contrarians, like the lawyer in Luke's gospel, who knew very well who his neighbor was, but wanted to justify himself and asked, "And who is my neighbour?"[1] Playing the Devil's advocate is an innate part of their character. These sorts of people will argue just for the sake of arguing.

Whatever the case, there are common questions, scenarios, and objections that come up frequently enough that I

---

1. Lk. 10:25-29.

thought it wise to take a moment to answer them, just to tie up some loose ends.

What is Love?

One of the biggest questions I encounter is, "What is love?" What does it actually mean to love someone in a Biblical sense?

In our modern world, we often associate love with feelings or emotions. You might think of love in the way that one might feel for a spouse or other romantic attachment. Perhaps love, to you, is the deep bond one has for a parent, child or sibling. Or maybe you think of love as the brotherly or sisterly bond that forms between childhood friends.

In all such comprehensions of love, people find it incredibly difficult to wrap their minds around the notion of having to manifest what would essentially be artificial feelings for everyone they encounter. This especially includes strangers whom they've never met, or those whom they might consider an enemy. While we are all capable of being kind, polite, etc., we can't make ourselves feel emotions for people that we don't actually have. The very thought of trying to do so is enough to give anyone a headache.

Furthermore, the idea that love is enough, that it fulfills the law, makes some people believe that sin is being redefined, or marginalized. I once even had a gentleman pack up and leave a Bible study because he was so flustered and offended by the notion of love over law that he couldn't continue with the conversation. He would say, "What about, 'you shall not steal'?" And I would respond, "If you have love, you won't steal." But he couldn't understand this. He was convinced that Christians walking in love alone would run amok without the law to restrict them.

But such frustrations and disagreements are founded in a misunderstanding of what love is. Love is not a feeling, but an action. It is a deliberate decision. Love is choosing to show kindness and charity to someone whether you like them or not. Love is doing the right thing. It is blessing or forgiving someone who did you wrong, even though they don't deserve it. Love is suffering a wrong and choosing not to seek retribution. That is how we are able to love both our friends and our enemies, and the stranger whom we have never met.[1] True love is deeds and decisions, not feelings or emotions.[2] Our enemies wouldn't be our enemies if we liked them.[3] You can love someone you emotionally contemn, as you can likewise hate someone you emotionally love. How we feel is how we feel, and there's not much we can do about that. But love — in decision, attitude, and deed — is absolutely controllable, regardless of our feelings. Love is magnanimity, charity, forgiveness, empathy, equity, etc., and has little to do with our emotions.[4]

From that perspective, it's readily apparent how love is the foundation upon which all the law was built. Pretty much every law can be traced back to the same principle. We don't steal because we wouldn't want someone to steal from us — do unto others. We don't commit adultery because we wouldn't want someone being with our spouse — do unto

---

1. Matt. 5:43-46.
2. 1 Jn. 3:18.
3. Matt. 5:44.
4. 1 Jn. 3:17-18; cf. Jas. 2:15-16.

others. Love is choosing to do the morally right thing in any given situation *to* people, *by* people, and *for* people. Love is righteousness. Thus, the basis of the law, whether it instructs us not to trip blind people, or to not reap every ear of corn in the field at harvest for the sake of the poor, is borne of neighborly love.[1]

As Jesus said, do to others as you would have them do to you. This *is* the law and the prophets.

It's Too Easy

Relative to the simplicity of love, I've heard it remarked quite a few times that the conclusions I've presented in this book sound just a little too easy. And I confess that I myself thought the same thing when the epiphany of how it worked first hit me. Believing in Jesus Christ and doing right by the people we come into contact with just isn't that hard. It almost carries the characteristic of "if it's too good to be true …" I even remember saying to myself, "Can that really be all there is to it?"

Truth be told, it's so easy that, whereas I used to think that living up to God's expectations was impossible, understanding the true gospel principle made me think quite the opposite. How could we *not* live up to his expectations?

In fact, Peter and Paul both comment about the reality of the freedom we now have. It's so free that they felt the need to admonish us not to let our freedom be an excuse for vice. Not all things are expedient or edifying, even if they

---

1. Lev. 19:14; 23:22.

are lawful.[1] Vice leads to sin, as in the case of strong drink, for example, that causes us to "drink, and forget the law, and pervert the judgment of any of the afflicted."[2] It's not the booze that's the problem, but the way we act when we drink it. Nothing is unclean of itself.[3]

This is why one man can eat all things, while another eats only herbs, or why one man can esteem a single day above all others, while another esteems every day alike.[4] A definitive law is not so arbitrary. If there was an absolute rule of law, the same law would apply to all in the same way. Clearly this is not the case. Whether you eat the meat or don't, esteem the day or don't, by faith you do it all to God.[5] It is conscience driven, relative to the strength of our faith, and not a matter of law.[6]

Make no mistake, it is mainstream Christianity, not the Bible, that has made a sin of nearly anything and everything you can imagine, from cupcakes being sinful for overweight people, to television being idolatry for football fans.

Sin is the failure to love, and nothing more, whether by deed, or lack thereof.[7] As Jesus says, "if ye can receive it," this is the truth of the matter.[8] His commandments are not

---

1. 1 Pet. 2:15-17; Gal. 5:1, 13-14; 1 Cor. 6:12, 10:23.
2. Prov. 31:4-5.
3. Rom. 14:22, 14:14.
4. Rom. 14:2, 5.
5. Rom. 14:6-8.
6. Rom. 14:1, 12; 1 Cor. 8:7-13, 10:29-31.
7. 1 Jn. 3:4; Matt. 7:12, 22:37-40; Rom. 13:8-10; Heb. 10:9; Jas. 4:17; Col. 2:14; Eph. 2:15-16. Sin is a transgression of the law, and the law is love. The old law, which is gone, was based on and fulfilled by love. The new law *is* love.
8. Matt. 19:11. I am not referencing the context, but the principle, which is that

difficult.[1] It really is that easy.

I Thought the New Testament was Harder

In the same vein of thought, one very common perception I run into is the presumption that "the New Testament is harder," or that "Jesus added to it, making it even more difficult." The previous topic, that it all sounds too easy, rides on the shoulders of this greater confusion, which, like so many other concepts, was a difficulty I once shared.

Bearing in mind the full context of the New Testament, let me be forthcoming on this and say up front that the New Testament is not harder. It is easier. The law was burdensome and difficult to bear.[2] The New Covenant is not. Jesus says that his yoke is easy and his burden light.[3] John says that God's commandments are not difficult.[4] Only the Devil would propagate the lie that the New Covenant is an infinitely more difficult version of the law, when the scriptures teach us that we are not under the law at all, but under grace.[5] The law, for us, even in its "less difficult" version, is failure

---

not everyone can receive difficult understandings. Time, study, and humility brings everything to light in due season.

1. 1 Jn. 5:3.
2. Gen. 4:7.
3. Matt. 11:28-30.
4. 1 Jn. 5:2-3.
5. Gal. 2:21, 3:1, 3:10, 5:2-4; Rom. 6:14; Acts 15:11; Eph. 2:5, 8; 2 Tim. 1:9. To be subject to the law makes Christ's sacrifice in vain. It will profit us nothing. He is of no effect to us. We are fallen from grace. And since we are saved by grace (Acts 15:11; Eph. 2:5, 8; 2 Tim. 1:9), to be fallen from grace is to be condemned. To be taught that we are under the law is to be "bewitched."

and condemnation, whereas the scriptures teach us that we are more than conquerors, and that we have overcome the adversary by our faith.[1]

As best as I have been able to discern from my many conversations, this idea that the New Testament is more difficult originates primarily, though not necessarily exclusively, from a few of the statements in the sermon on the mount, in which there appears to be a number of augmentations to the commandments.[2] The law says that you shall not kill, but to be angry with your brother without cause puts you in equal danger of hell fire.[3] The law says that you shall not commit adultery, but if you look at a woman with lust, you've already committed adultery with her.[4] Such instances where people have perceived expansions on the commandments have led to a wide-spread and self-condemning belief that every thought in your head, every emotion that grips your heart, and every physical reaction of your body is sin. And, admittedly, from that perspective, it's hard to argue with the notion that Christ made things harder.

However, commandments like those mentioned, along with everything else Jesus talked about in the sermon, are summed up with the golden rule. "Therefore," he says, as a conclusion to the sermon, "all things whatsoever ye would that men should do to you, do ye even so to them: for this is the law and the prophets."[5] All the alleged additions are

---

1. Heb. 7:18-19, 8:6-8; Rom. 3:19-20, 4:15, 7:7-13, 8:37; 1 Jn. 2:12-14, 5:4-5.
2. Matt. 5:21-48.
3. Matt. 5:21-22; 1 Jn. 3:11-12, 14-15.
4. Matt. 5:27-28.
5. Matt. 7:12.

merely principle explanations. Paul goes on and on about the spirit of the law versus the letter of the law. Jesus is just preaching the spirit of the law; love your neighbor as yourself. Paul reiterates this same truth in Romans.[1] The fact is, you can keep the law to the letter while violating the very principle upon which it was founded. The same cannot be said about the reverse. If you live according to the principle, you will live up to the full intent of the letter.[2]

So to understand the "expansions" of the sermon, you have to view them in the correct light. To be angry without cause is simply malice, borne out of envy. Cain was "wroth," or angry, because Abel's offering was accepted while his was not. But Cain still had the opportunity to do rightly. Sin merely laid in wait.[3] Paul says to be angry and sin not, which clearly separates anger and sin.[4] It is not anger or dissatisfaction that's a problem, but unjustified anger, and the actions associated with it. Cain's "anger" is equated to hate by John, and it led to murder, whereas, "the message that [we] heard from the beginning [is] that we should love one another," and "love worketh no ill to his neighbour."[5] Ergo, whosoever is angry with his brother without a cause shall be *in danger* of the judgment.[6] Unjustified anger leads to wickedness. We must master it.[7] If you have an issue with someone, make it

---

1. Rom. 13:9-10.
2. Rom. 9:30-32, 13:8-10; 2 Cor. 3:6-11.
3. Gen. 4:5-6.
4. Eph. 4:26.
5. 1 Jn. 3:11-12, 14-15; Rom. 13:10.
6. Matt. 5:22.
7. Matt. 5:21-22; 1 Jn. 3:11-12, 14-15.

right. If you know someone has an issue with you, make it right.[1] Don't let the sun go down on your wrath.[2]

Christ is not telling us we can't be angry from time to time. He himself was angry on occasion.[3] He's telling us not to hold grudges, not to give someone else an excuse to hold a grudge against us, and not to hate people. He's telling us to put away malice.[4] There's no reason whatsoever that we should wish or attempt ill on someone else. If you maintain a mindset of brotherly love, Christ's message in this regard is not a difficult thing to understand or live up to.

Concerning the adultery and lust issue, the confusion is even more severe. The common understanding of this passage leans towards sexual immorality of the mind, and has become an enormous stumbling block, especially for young men. Going back to my earliest days as a Christian, I remember being sixteen or seventeen years old. And for me and my friend, our understanding, as it was taught to us, was that we were committing adultery if the right girl in the right clothes made us think about sex for even the most fleeting of moments. I remember sharing the gospel at the Ft. Lauderdale beach with the youth group, and my friend and I spent the better part of the day making the joke, "I don't see her. Or her. Or her," as we'd hold our hands up to our eyes to block the view of young women in scant bikinis.

Although we should not seek to deliberately indulge

---

1. Matt. 5:23-24.
2. Eph. 4:26.
3. Matt. 21:18-19, 23:13-39; Mk. 3:5, 11:12-14; Lk. 11:37-52; Jn. 2:15-16.
4. Eph. 4:31; Col. 3:8; Jas. 5:9. It's important to note that Jesus specified being angry "without cause."

such appetites, and should certainly strive to dwell on more appropriate thoughts, this common interpretation is about as far from what Christ meant as a thing could be.[1]

To understand what he's saying here, there are a few things that need to be understood. Jesus' statement is loaded with implicit colloquialisms, masked by language barriers and two thousand years of cultural evolution. I may have to explain it to you, but he didn't need to explain it to them. They understood exactly what he meant.

First and foremost, the context is adultery, not random sexual desire. This context doesn't change after the initial statement, but is defined by it. While Christ may be elaborating on what constitutes culpability, he is still nevertheless talking about *adultery*. And adultery, to those listening to him speak, was the crime of a man taking another man's wife. Due to the polygamist culture of first century Judaism, the man's marital status was immaterial to the scenario.[2] A married man who took another woman simply had an extra wife. But if the man took a woman who was already married, then it was the crime of adultery, whether due to the woman's lack of fidelity, or the man's presumptuousness in taking what belonged to his neighbor. Either way, the woman in the scenario had to be married for adultery to occur, while for the man it didn't matter. It is only in our Romanized perspective of monogamy that a cheating husband

---

1. 2 Cor. 10:5; Phil. 4:8.
2. Matt. 5:27; Joseph. *AJ* 17.14, 20.259-267; Justin *1 Apol.* 134. Josephus, writing during the reign of Domitian, confirms the continued and accepted practice amongst the Jews to have multiple wives. Justin Martyr confirms that this continued to be the case.

is considered an adulterer.

The second point is the use and interpretation of the word "lust." By definition, this English word merely refers to desire, and if the passage is interpreted according to that definition, the translation is accurate, if weak. The problem is that "lust" carries with it the connotation of *sexual* desire in our own usage, causing most to mistakenly interpret this as a crime of mental fornication, which is unilaterally applied to any and all women, regardless of whether they are married or not. You see her, like her, are sexually attracted to her ... you've had sex with her in your heart, which constitutes adultery by the strict interpretive understanding of the passage. However, the Greek word ἐπιθυμέω, from which "lust" has been translated, is also used by Paul in Romans 13:9 when listing the Ten Commandments, saying, "Thou shalt not covet (ἐπιθυμέω)," whereas his intent to portray sexual desire or passion employs the word πυρόω in 1 Corinthians 7:9. Better to marry than to burn (πυρόω).

What Jesus is associating with adultery here is the "coveting" of your neighbor's wife. And covetousness is not necessarily sexual. Nor is it merely "to want" or "to desire" in the basest form. We all "want" things. That is the foundation of trade and commerce. Supply and demand. You "want," and someone else "provides." This is basic economics. I grow corn. You grow oranges. I "want" your oranges, and so we trade. I have not "coveted" my neighbor's oranges.

For "you shall not covet" to be fulfilled by "love your neighbor as yourself," as Paul says that it is, covetousness must, by necessity, affect your neighbor.[1] And if it affects

---

1. Rom. 3:8-10.

your neighbor, then it must have an outward manifestation that can be quantified. Love for your neighbor would have no bearing on the sin otherwise. The desires in our hearts and the thoughts in our heads do no ill until we choose to act upon them. So, to covet is not merely "to want," which your neighbor will never know or suffer by, but to want something to such a degree that we attempt to obtain it, which *does* harm them. Thus, to set your sights upon another man's wife to "covet" her is to seek to obtain her.

Ergo, what Jesus is saying concerning adultery is that while the law says, "you shall not commit adultery," if you *try* to take her, the attempt makes you just as guilty. The effort is equal to the act, whether you succeed or not. Thus, it's not the surreptitious look or the sexual thought that's the problem, but the witty joke or inappropriate touch with the motive of eliciting a reciprocated attraction. In other words, it has nothing to do with them inadvertently attracting your attention, but about you deliberately attracting theirs to win their affection. That is what it is to covet your neighbor's spouse, boyfriend, or girlfriend.

To reiterate, it is not my intent to suggest that it is okay for us to seek out or dwell on carnal things. All I'm saying is that that's not what Christ is saying here. He's telling us that to try to take someone's wife — or husband, boyfriend, or girlfriend — is the same as actually doing so.

So understand that Jesus didn't make the New Testament more difficult. This perception only exists in a vacuum. It is built upon the assumptions that we still have the law, and that the law has been expanded upon. In reality, we no longer have the law, and Jesus was actually just elaborating on the functional principle of the law, which is love. The moment one accepts that the law has been abolished, the difficulty resolves itself.

We Don't Have to be Sinners

The final point I'd like to make is that by a proper understanding of love and its simplicity, we can live up to God's expectations. It is a great misconception, and one that has become something of a personal pet peeve to me, that we, as Christians, are still sinners, and will always *be* sinners. Some are even given to believe that we can't go so much as a single day without sinning. And this notion is taught and believed by people at all levels, up to and including the pulpit, and even in the seminaries.

To this, I will boldly state that this couldn't be further from the truth. John says that those abiding in God do *not* sin, and although he allows for the exception, he tells us that it's simply not in our nature. We are born of God.[1]

While we may err in weakness, the dedicated Christian typically goes through their day, day by day, not sinning at all. The mentality of perpetual sinfulness is borne out of the notion that, again, the New Testament is more difficult. People have been taught that where we once had the law, we

---

1. 1 Jn. 3:6, 2:1-2, 3:9. Please note here that I do not subscribe to the idea of absolute sinless perfection. While John does state that those abiding in God do not sin, and that we are unable to sin because we are born of God, he does make the concession that we have an advocate if we do sin, admitting by default that his statements in 3:6-9 are not absolutes, but general principles. It's not that we can't physically commit sin. It's that Christians just don't behave that way. Sin is the exception rather than the rule, whereas mainstream Christianity teaches the opposite.

now we have the law on steroids. Thoughts are sinful. Emotions are sinful. What you eat or drink is sinful. Your entertainment is sinful. *Every*thing is sinful!

But this mentality is the absolute antithesis of what Christ accomplished and what the Bible teaches. Thoughts are not sin. They are thoughts. And we should cast down imaginations, and every high thing that exalts itself against the knowledge of God, and bring every thought into captivity to the obedience of Christ.[1] Emotions are not sin. We can be angry and not sin.[2] What we eat and drink is not sin. It's not what goes in the mouth that defiles us, but what comes out.[3] If we want to enjoy that dreadful and idolatrous football game, we are free to do exactly that, being a thing that is amongst the good of our labor. It is the gift of God that we should eat our bread with joy, and drink our wine with a merry heart, and that we should make our soul enjoy the good of all our labour that we perform all the days of our lives, for God accepts our works.[4]

I don't criticize these things lightly, mind you. Many of them were once my own point of view, right alongside so many others. Whether it was a bad thought, a pretty girl that inspired carnal thoughts, or a dirty word that slipped past my lips, I just couldn't live up to the impossible standard that I had been taught to believe was the New Testament.

And then everything changed.

Know this: We are not failures in Jesus Christ. Only the

---

1. 2 Cor. 10:5.
2. Eph. 4:26.
3. Matt. 15:17-19.
4. Eccl. 2:24, 3:13, 5:18-19, 8:15, 9:7-9.

Devil would try to convince you that you are. You don't have to be a sinner. In fact, you *shouldn't* be a sinner. You've been given everything you need to live a righteous life, free of sin. Love is the key.[1] It is the commandment of Christ.[2] And it is most certainly an expected, and attainable, behavior.[3] Anyone telling you otherwise does not understand.[4] As Paul says, we should "awake to righteousness and sin not." Our failure to understand this stems from a lack in our knowledge of God, and this is a shameful thing.[5]

If you love those around you, actively, by deed and decision, you are not sinning. This is a perpetual theme throughout the New Testament.

> Owe no man any thing, but to love one another: for he that loveth another hath fulfilled the law.[6]

> For all the law is fulfilled in one word, [even] in this; Thou shalt love thy neighbour as thyself.[7]

> If ye fulfil the royal law according to the scripture, 'Thou shalt love thy neighbour as thyself,' ye do well.[8]

> He that loveth his brother abideth in the light, and there is

---

1. Gal. 5:14.
2. Jn. 13:34.
3. Rom. 6:1-2, 6:15-16; 1 Pet. 4:1-2.
4. 1 Cor. 15:34; 1 Jn. 3:7-8.
5. 1 Cor. 15:34.
6. Rom. 13:8.
7. Gal. 5:14.
8. Jas. 2:8.

none occasion of stumbling in him.[1]

> And beside this, giving all diligence, add to your faith virtue; and to virtue knowledge; And to knowledge temperance; and to temperance patience; and to patience godliness; And to godliness brotherly kindness; and to brotherly kindness charity. [...] for if ye do these things, ye shall never fall.[2]

You can even see this teaching in the writings of the early church fathers. Polycarp, for example, was a disciple of the Apostle John.[3] In his letter to the Philippians, he says:

> For if any one be inwardly possessed of these graces, he hath fulfilled the command of righteousness, since he that hath love is far from all sin.[4]

Love is the point. It will always be the point. Love never fails. The hardest part of living up to God's expectations is convincing Christians to accept the *simplicity* that is love. They are determined to make things more complicated than they need to be. Love those around you, in deed and in truth.[5] This is the expected behavior. This is how people will know that we are Christ's disciples. Do this, and you will not fail.

---

1. 1 Jn. 2:5.
2. 2 Pet. 5:10.
3. Euseb. *Hist. eccl.* 5.20.6; Iren. *Ad. Haer.* 3.3.4, 5.33.4.
4. Poly. *Phil.* 3; cf. 1 Jn. 2:10; 2 Pet. 1:3-10, v. 10 esp.
5. 1 Jn. 3:18.

8

A Call to Action

At this point, it's time for me to call you to action. Faith provokes deed. While our salvation is the free gift of God's grace, not acquired by our works of righteousness, we were nevertheless preordained by God to be created in Jesus Christ for the purpose of performing those good works.[1] Our continuing faith is defined and demonstrated by our actions. As James says, the body without the spirit is dead, just as faith without works is dead.[2] As a Christian, if you don't have the works, then your faith counts for naught.[3] Faith is not merely hope or belief. It is the *evidence* of things not seen.[4] And sitting around on the couch all day *believing* is evidence of nothing at all. Even the devils believe and tremble.[5] This is why James says, "show me thy faith without thy

---

1. Eph. 2:8-10.
2. Jms. 2:20, 26.
3. Jms. 2:20; 1 Cor. 13:1-3.
4. Heb. 11:1.
5. Jms. 2:19.

A Call to Action

works, and I will show thee my faith by my works."[1]

Of all the disputes in modern Christendom, faith versus works ranks in the top two, second only to whether or not we need to keep the law of Moses. Is it faith, or is it works? We're saved by faith, without works.[2] But faith without works is dead.[3]

The problem concerning this issue, from my own personal observation, is that people tend to treat faith and works as though they are juxtaposed rather than symbiotic. The arguments tend towards one extreme or the other. Those who insist that works are necessary are scorned by those who think it's by faith alone. At the same time, those who say it is by faith alone are rebuked by those who say that faith without works is dead. But faith and works are complementary, not synonymous. Faith progresses to works. The second is borne of the first. And so the arguments themselves, at their foundation, are not even the same, though this truth seems to escape most people's notice.

Works don't save you.[4] Ever. Whether you are pious and a doer of righteous deeds, or a wicked person mired in sin, we are all on even ground in receiving the gift of salvation.[5] None of us are worthy.[6] We've all sinned.[7] God saves us by

---

1. Jms. 2:18.
2. Rom. 3:20; Eph. 2:8-9.
3. Jms. 2:20.
4. Rom. 3:20; Eph. 2:8-9.
5. Rom. 3:22, 5:6-8.
6. Rev. 5:2-3.
7. Rom. 3:23.

his good grace when we confess our sins, profess Christ, believe, and are baptized.[1] "Works" carries the implication of wages or privileges due. "Because I performed this work, I *earned* salvation." "Because I did this thing, I *deserve* salvation." Apart from the physical acts of *acceptance* mentioned above — to confess, profess, believe, and be baptized — which by their very nature fall outside of the scope and context of works with expectation of gain or privilege, there is no work we can do by which we can claim to have earned or deserved salvation.[2] We are saved by faith, and faith alone.

But our faith, once we have *become* Christians, carries with it the requirement of evincing good works.[3] Faith without works is dead.[4] While it may take some time for you to learn and grow as a Christian, if you are sincere, your faith will inevitably produce the fruits of the spirit; love, joy, peace, longsuffering, gentleness, goodness, faith, meekness,

---

1. Rom. 10:9-11; Matt. 28:19; Mk. 16:16. The scriptures state that those who believe and are baptized will be saved. While I recognize that many debate whether this means spiritual or water baptism, and some even disregard baptism altogether, or treat it as optional, the position of this work is that baptism is directly stated as being part of the equation. It is symbolic of our burial and resurrection with Christ (Rom. 6:4; Col. 2:12). The example in Acts 8:26-40 also demonstrates an apostolic practice of water baptism beyond dispute. The eunuch from Ethiopia is reading Isaiah. Philip explains the scripture of prophecy to him, then preaches to him the gospel and Jesus Christ. When they encounter water, the eunuch asks, "See, *here is* water; what doth hinder me to be baptized?" Isaiah didn't impart the notion of water baptism. That clearly came from Philip in his sharing of the gospel. As a result, "they went down both into the water, both Philip and the eunuch; and he baptized him."

2. Rom. 3:20, 4:4; Eph. 2:8-9.

3. Eph. 2:8-10.

4. Jms. 2:20, 26.

temperance.[1] It is a natural evolution. To faith is added virtue, and to virtue is added knowledge, and to knowledge is added temperance, and to temperance is added patience, and to patience is added godliness, and to godliness is added brotherly kindness, and to brotherly kindness is added charity, or love.[2] If we have and do these things, we will never fall.[3] But if we lack these things, we are blind.[4] Love is the pinnacle of our spiritual maturity. It's what it all leads up to.

It is not a coincidence that James makes his argument for works within the context and framework of love. "If a brother or sister be naked, and destitute of daily food," James says, "And one of you say unto them, Depart in peace, be *ye* warmed and filled; notwithstanding ye give them not those things which are needful to the body; what *doth it* profit?"[5] Therefore ... "show me thy faith without thy works, and I will show thee my faith by my works."[6]

Thus, James is here challenging the evidence of faith in the absence of a person's works of love, and not merely the "works of righteousness," which Paul so often refers to as having nothing to do with salvation. Works of love are part and parcel to our faith. Even Paul agrees with this truth, saying, "For in Jesus Christ neither circumcision availeth any thing, nor uncircumcision; but faith which worketh by

---

1. Gal. 5:22-23.
2. 2 Pet. 1:5-7.
3. 2 Pet. 1:8, 10.
4. 2 Pet. 1:9.
5. Jms. 2:14-17.
6. Jms. 2:18.

love."[1] Faith, using James' example, is demonstrated in giving that brother or sister the things that are needful to the body. Your labor of love becomes the visible *evidence* of the faith you have in the invisible God, whereas the argument that belief alone is adequate neglects the love to which we have been charged.[2]

So understand that there is no conflict in ideas between James and Paul. They are preaching the same thing. Our faith requires the works of love.[3] If you try to be righteous by the law, but fail in any point, you are a transgressor.[4] Though you have the faith to move mountains, you are nothing if you do not have love.[5] Your faith is dead.[6] But if you fulfill the law by walking according to the spirit, or principle of the law, loving your neighbor as yourself, you do well.[7]

Again, it's the same message.

Further, we can see the same thing from John. Of all the apostles, he is the most black and white on the subject. There is no gray area with him. Either you love, or you do not. You either know God, or you do not.[8] You dwell in God, or you do not.[9] You can love those around you and abide in the light, have no reason to stumble, be without fear, and have his love

---

1. Gal. 5:6; cf. Rom. 12:10, 13:8; 2 Cor. 6:6; Gal. 5:13; Eph. 5:2; 1 Thes. 1:3.
2. Jn. 13:34-35.
3. Gal. 5:6; Rom. 12:10, 13:8; 2 Cor. 6:6; Gal. 5:13; Eph. 5:2; 1 Thes. 1:3.
4. Jms. 2:10-11; Gal. 5:3-4.
5. 1 Cor. 13:2.
6. Jms. 2:10-11
7. Rom. 7:6, 8:1-2, 13:8-10; 2 Cor. 3:6; Gal. 5:14; Jms. 2:8.
8. 1 Jn. 4:7-8.
9. 1 Jn. 3:17; Jms. 2:14-17; 1 Jn. 4:12, 16, 3:10.

perfected in you.[1] Else, you can choose not to love those around you and walk in darkness, abide in death, be void of the love of God, be branded a liar, and likened to a murderer.[2]

Suffice it to say, John doesn't pull any punches.

But recognize that John is making the same argument. The only difference between him, James, and Paul, is that John doesn't make a distinction between works and faith. It's all wrapped up in a single package, and he's very cut and dry about it. If you aren't doing the works of love, you're a liar to say that you know God.[3]

Nowhere is this more pointedly illustrated than by Christ himself.

> Then shall he say also unto them on the left hand, Depart from me, ye cursed, into everlasting fire, prepared for the devil and his angels: For I was an hungered, and ye gave me no meat: I was thirsty, and ye gave me no drink: I was a stranger, and ye took me not in: naked, and ye clothed me not: sick, and in prison, and ye visited me not. Then shall they also answer him, saying, Lord, when saw we thee an hungered, or athirst, or a stranger, or naked, or sick, or in prison, and did not minister unto thee? Then shall he answer them, saying, Verily I say unto you, Inasmuch as ye did *it* not to one of the least of these, ye did *it* not to me.[4]

Please note here that Jesus does not say, "I was in the synagogue and saw you not," but that he was hungry and we

---

1. 1 Jn. 2:10, 4:12, 16, 18.
2. 1 Jn. 2:11, 3:14, 4:20, 3:15.
3. 1 Jn. 4:7-8.
4. Matt. 25:41-45.

didn't feed him. His gripe is not about ritualistic deeds, but about the labor of love that is absent.

So understand that saying a sinner's prayer, or being baptized, is not enough. Not everyone that says to him, "Lord, Lord," shall enter into the kingdom of heaven.[1] Through the heart we believe, and are made righteous. With our mouth we confess and are saved.[2] By baptism we are buried with Christ and resurrected in the newness of life.[3] It is a free gift from God, not acquired by our works, but by the grace of God through our faith. But as new creations, we have to repent and live the life of a Christian.[4] It is our purpose in Christ.[5] If we do not lead a life of love, then our professed faith is a lie.[6] Our love is how people will know that we are Christ's disciples.[7]

Our love is also a reflection of God. We are supposed to be a light to the world, and we have to be mindful not to behave in a way that tarnishes the gospel, but that illuminates it.[8] While many have discovered that love is the key to our daily walk, there are many others who would just as readily flip someone the bird coming out of the church parking lot, road-raging because they are impatient to get to the restaurant. There are churches that minister to the needy, whose

---

1. Matt. 7:19.
2. Rom. 10:9-11.
3. Rom. 6:4; Col. 2:12.
4. Acts 2:38.
5. Eph. 2:8-10.
6. 1 Jn. 2:4, 4:20.
7. 1 Jn. 3:23; Jn. 13:34-35.
8. Matt. 5:14; 2 Cor. 6:3.

pastors are humble. And there are churches where a new gym takes priority over charity, or where the pastor doesn't seem to understand the principle of being "content with food and raiment," or more simply, content with a modest lifestyle.[1]

In the first few centuries of our faith, Christians were being killed without mercy, and our numbers grew because of their extraordinary faith. They offered their necks to the lions, and entered the arena singing hymns, and praising God.[2] Christians shared everything in their communities.[3] They ministered to the sick, homeless, and hungry. And our numbers grew because of their charity. Christian behavior was so godly that it even broke the cycle of hatred in some instances, as in the time of the emperor Maximinus, when famine and pestilence ravaged Rome. The heathen glorified God because of the piety and zeal of the Christians, who were the only ones to stay in the city and minister to the sick and hungry.[4] Their love, charity, and faith was intoxicating. People wanted what they had. And so our numbers swelled.

Today, people run from Christianity because we lack the same faith, love, and humility. People don't want to be a part of what the church has become. There are Christians who stand on street corners and shout to passersby that they're going to hell. There are Christians who go to a restaurant on a Sunday afternoon after church, and have the gall to criticize the server for "working on the Sabbath," when it's their

---

[1]. 1 Tim. 6:6-9.
[2]. Euseb. *Hist. eccl.* 4.15.4-7.
[3]. Tert. *Apol.* 39.
[4]. Euseb. *Hist. eccl.* 9.8.11-14.

fault the server is having to work in the first place. We live in a world where names like Jim Bakker are still alive and well in the memory of many. Yet, there are pastors who still have the poor judgement of living a life of luxury, paid for at the expense of people who often enough can't pay their own utility bills. It's the widow's mite putting meat on the prince's plate. It's downright despicable. As Martin Luther complained in his *Ninety-Five Theses*, when it was said that the poor were the treasure of the church, it's not a thing that should be taken literally.[1]

To the average non-Christian, we are a faith of scandals, greed, hypocrisy, arrogance, and even hatred. And while I would love to say that it's not really true, the perception is real enough that even Christian contemporary bands sing about it, like Casting Crowns. "If we are the body, why aren't his arms reaching? Why aren't his hands healing? Why aren't his words teaching? If we are the body, why aren't his feet going? Why is his love not showing them there is a way?" And their song is by no means the only one out there. Such songs exist because we all know the kind of things that go on in church. It's been going on at least as long as I've been a Christian.

It's time that changed.

Never forget that you might be the only image of Jesus Christ a person ever sees. While it goes without saying that people can and will disappoint you, we should endeavor to be the image of Christ on earth. At some point in your Christian walk, *you* will be the inspiration for someone else. At some point, *you* are going to be the person someone else

---

1. M. Luther, *Ninety-five Theses*, no. 59.

A Call to Action

looks up to, looks to for answers, and whom someone else will try to emulate or impress. What you do matters!

To this day, I still use a Ryrie Study Bible because of the guy who took the time to mentor and disciple me in the weightier teachings of scripture. While I presently find the Ryrie to be somewhat fundamental and simple compared to others I've come across over the years, I still have one as my primary go-to Bible, and would likely buy another one if my current Bible fell into such disrepair that I needed to replace it. That's how much of an impact he made on me.

To this day, I still listen to certain music because of the girl who used to take me to church. She used to sing in the car, and was quite talented. I can still remember her singing *Lead Me On*, by Amy Grant, and *This Means War*, by Petra. Most of my earliest lessons in faith and encouragement came from her. She educated me in the basics and taught me not to over-burden myself by looking too far ahead. She didn't just bring me to church and get me converted. She discipled me, educated me, and made sure I made it to church every week. She did her Christian duty by me. Without her perseverance, I might never have gone back beyond that first time.

I still seek the praise of my first pastor, and those whose scriptural knowledge challenged me to learn more, and to rise to the standard of their admiration.

I can still remember the powerful obedience of a guy who broke off a bad relationship for the sake of his faith. I'll never forget how he cried outside on the curb at youth group, broken-hearted, because of the decision he had had to make. While I take no joy in the pain he suffered that night, his dedication taught me more than any sermon ever could.

I can't tell you what your own labors of love will be in

your daily walk. Only you can know. Maybe it'll be a homeless guy that you can gift with a meal. Or a single mother who needs help getting her car repaired, and you can help, either physically or financially. Perhaps there will be someone who needs help with their power bill, whether it be a stranger or a fellow congregation member. Maybe it's an obnoxious person you just need to forgive, and show by your humility that the way of God is better than anger. Maybe it's a new convert who needs your praise and encouragement, or for you to step up and disciple them. I honestly don't know. The Holy Spirit will guide you from one situation to the next. It's really not for me to say what choices will be laid before you, or how the circumstances will guide the decisions you have to make.

But whatever those decisions are, it is your duty as a Christian to show the love of Christ. If they're hungry, feed them. If they're naked, clothe them. If they seek knowledge, educate them. If they need comfort, comfort them. If they have a need, fulfill it.

That's what real faith does.

Never forget that we have been given a great commission. We are told to go into all the world and preach the gospel, and to teach the nations the things Christ taught us.[1] We weren't instructed to condemn the world and tell them they're going to hell. We weren't instructed to seclude ourselves in church, pretending to be holy on Sunday while turning a blind eye to the needs of others. We are lights on a hill, meant to be a beacon for all.

We were instructed to tell people about Jesus Christ, to

---

1. Matt. 28:19-20; Mk. 16:15.

behave rightly, and to love people. And we don't teach that with words alone. We teach it by example.

In the end, it is our obligation as Christians to believe on the name of Jesus Christ, the only begotten son of God, who died for our sins and rose again from the dead on the third day. It is to confess him openly, without shame or fear, and to lead others to do the same.[1] It is to have hope in the grace of God and the undeserved gift of salvation, and to share the good news of that gift with the world.[2] It is to love the Lord our God with all our heart, all our soul, all our mind, and all our strength.[3] And it is to love those around us, just as Christ loved us, in deed and in truth, which is the fruit and evidence of our faith, and the evidence to the world that we belong to Christ.[4] As Paul tells us, what remains is faith, hope, and love, though the greatest of these is love.[5]

This is what it is to be a Christian.

This is the gospel.[6]

---

1. 1 Jn. 3:23; Rom. 10:9.
2. Rom. 8:24-25, 15:14; Gal. 5:5; Eph. 4:4-6; Col. 1:23, 27; 1 Thes. 1:3; Heb. 7:19.
3. Matt. 22:37-39; Mk. 12:30-31; Lk. 10:27.
4. 1 Jn. 3:23; Jn. 13:34-35.
5. 1 Cor. 13:13.
6. 1 Pet. 1:18-25.

I hope this has been enlightening and edifying. I'm always open to discussion if you have questions. Feel free to email me at: alex.frazier@charter.net with S. Book in the Subject Line so it doesn't get missed amongst bills and spam. A good review on Amazon is also appreciated if you found the book worthy of comment. It lets other potential readers know that it is worth their time.

Blessings to you and yours.

Alex Frazier

www.ingramcontent.com/pod-product-compliance
Lightning Source LLC
Chambersburg PA
CBHW031402040426
42444CB00005B/390